Celtic Knots, Mandalas & Patterns

30 Colouring Pages

Volume 1

Lorraine Kelly

Lozs Art

lozsart.com

Twitter @lozsloot

Facebook LozsArt

DeviantArt - LorraineKelly

tumblr.com/blog/lozs-art

About the Artwork

Inspiration for the artwork comes from Celtic and Persian traditional art. Sacred geometry techniques underpin some of the designs. This book contains a mix of mandalas, tangled designs on top of geometric patterns, Celtic knots and Australian native flowers.

About Lorraine Kelly

Lorraine Kelly is a self-taught artist who lives in Western Australia. Originally, she worked in the finance industry in Perth, Western Australia. After marrying. she had a sea-change and moved to the South-West of Western Australia to raise their family. During this time, she began her own business on eBay selling her hand-painted glassware and craft items.

Since 2016 she has been creating and publishing adult coloring books.

Previous coloring books include:

Cetlic Knots Adult Coloring Book – 30 Coloring Pages,

Australian Birds Adult Coloring Book

Murder and Mystery: Penny Dreadfuls Adult Coloring Book, and since this book has published

Celtic Knots, Mandalas and Patterns: Volume 2

Note from the Author:

Please review this book if you enjoyed it, as it will help me greatly!

You can find more of my books and coloring pages at:

http://lozart.com.au

http://stores.ebay.com.au/lozsloot

https://www.etsy.com/au/shop/LozsArt

Search Lorraine T Kelly on Amazon.

Like LozsArt on Facebook to share your coloured pictures and to keep up to date with new books and offers.

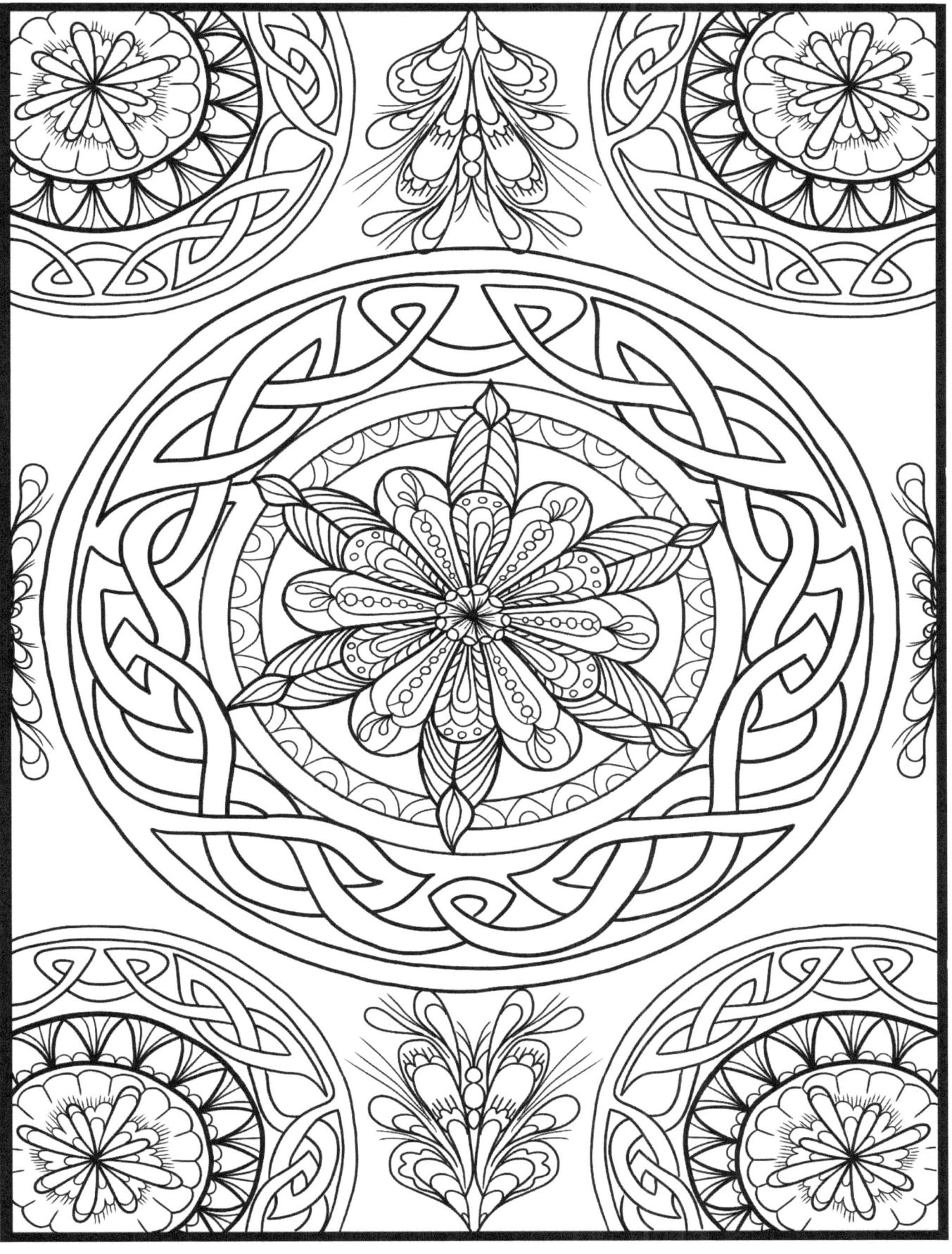

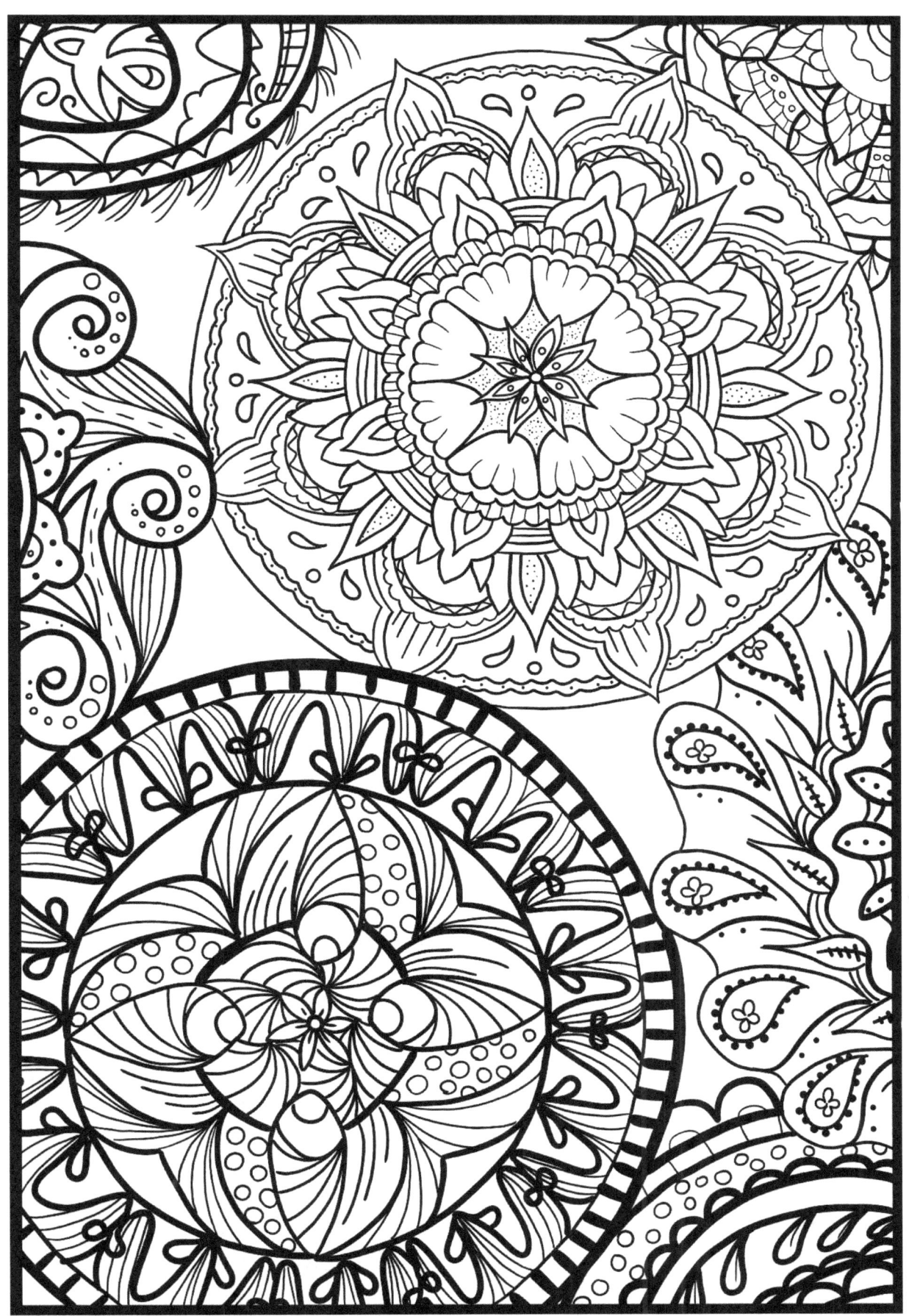

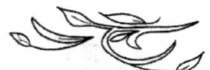

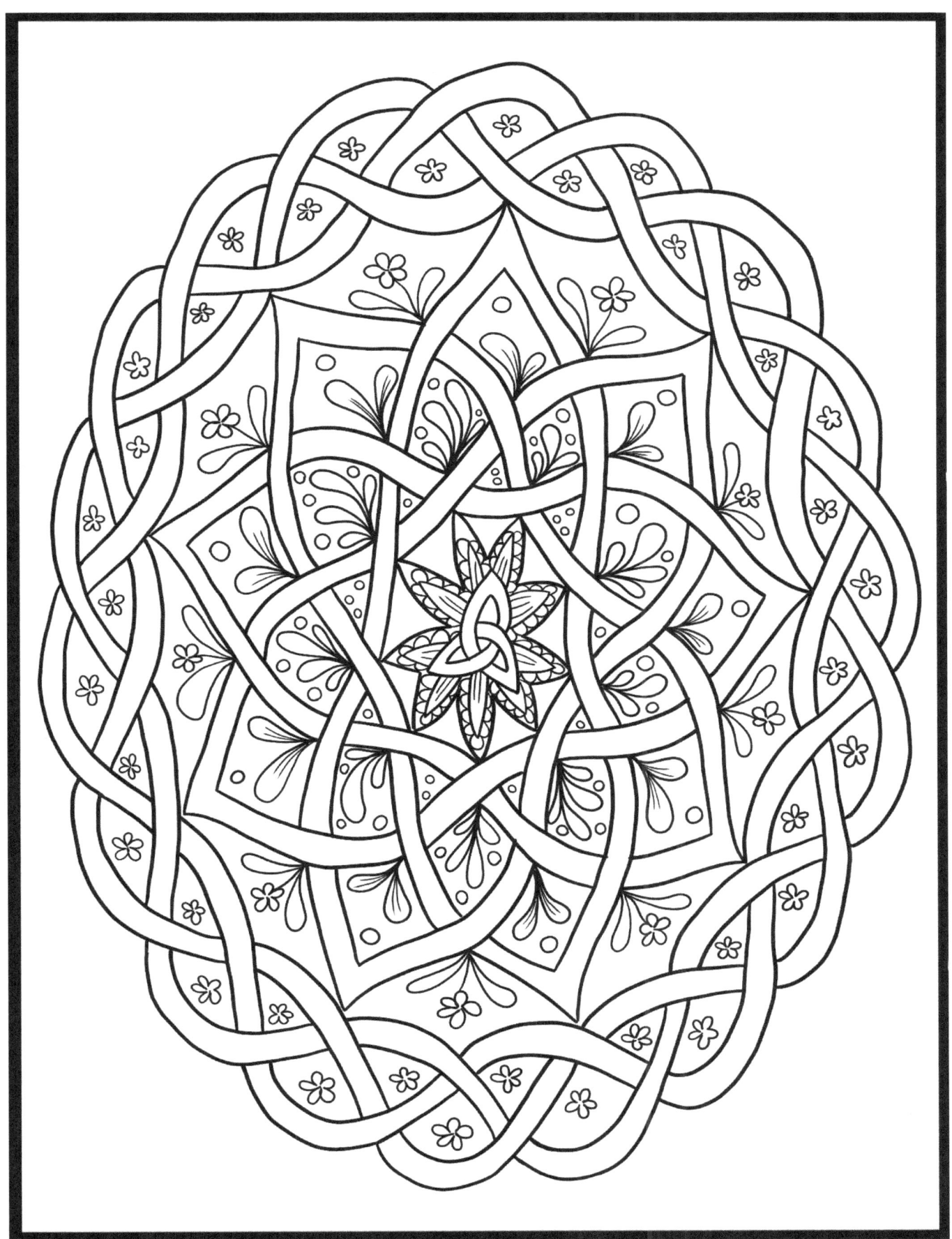

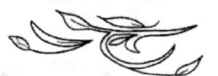

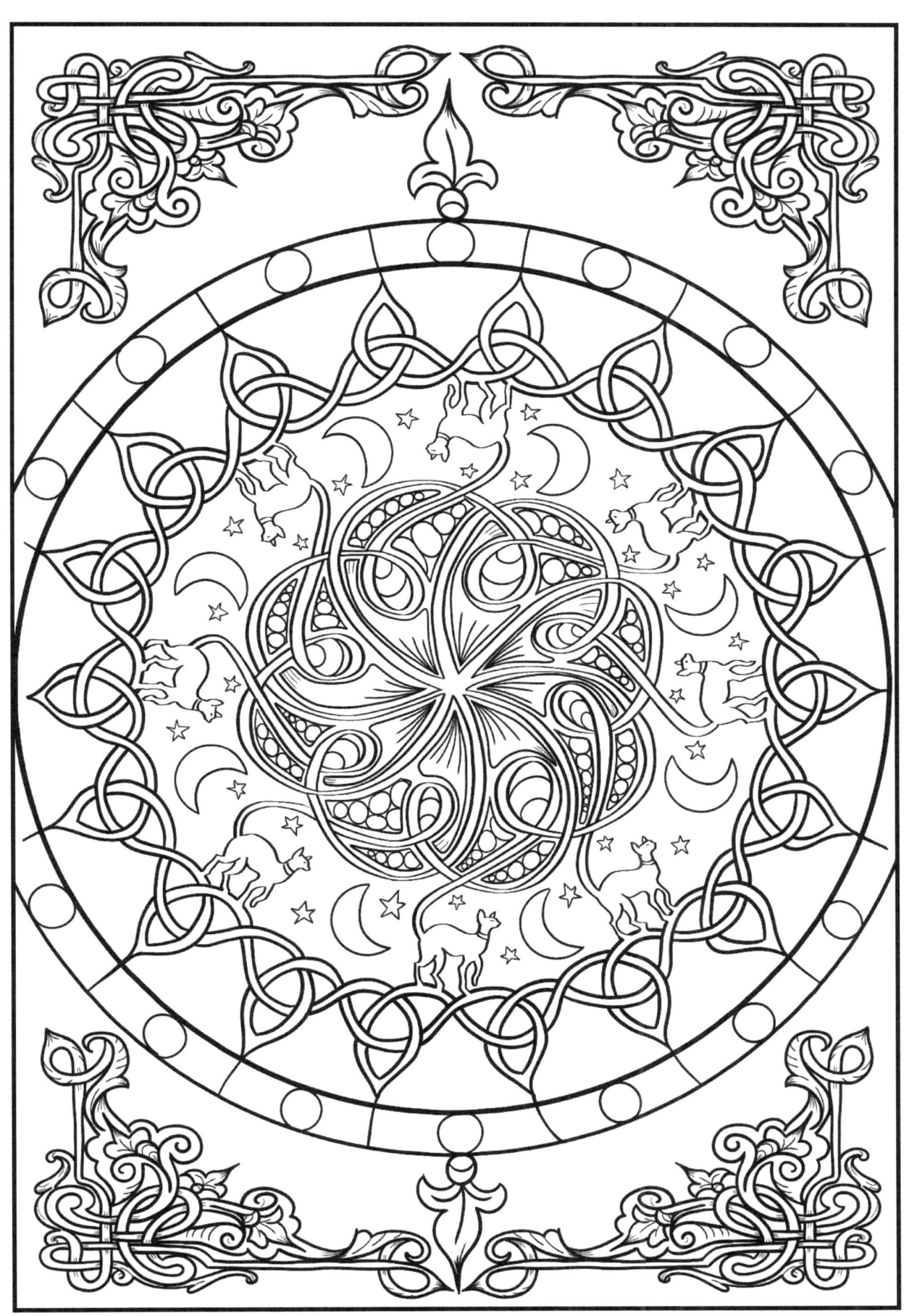

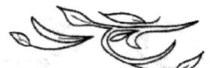

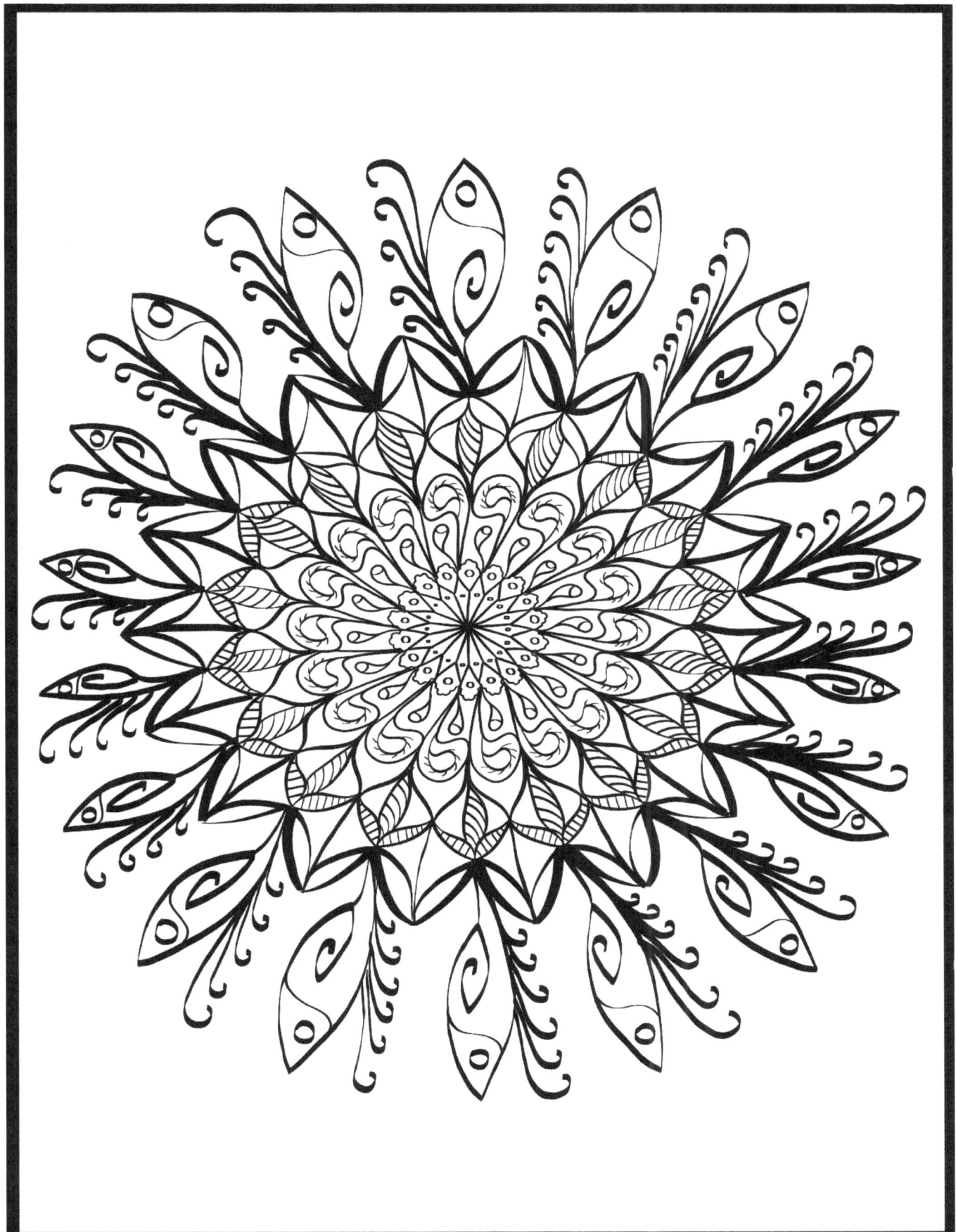

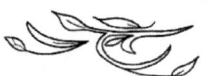

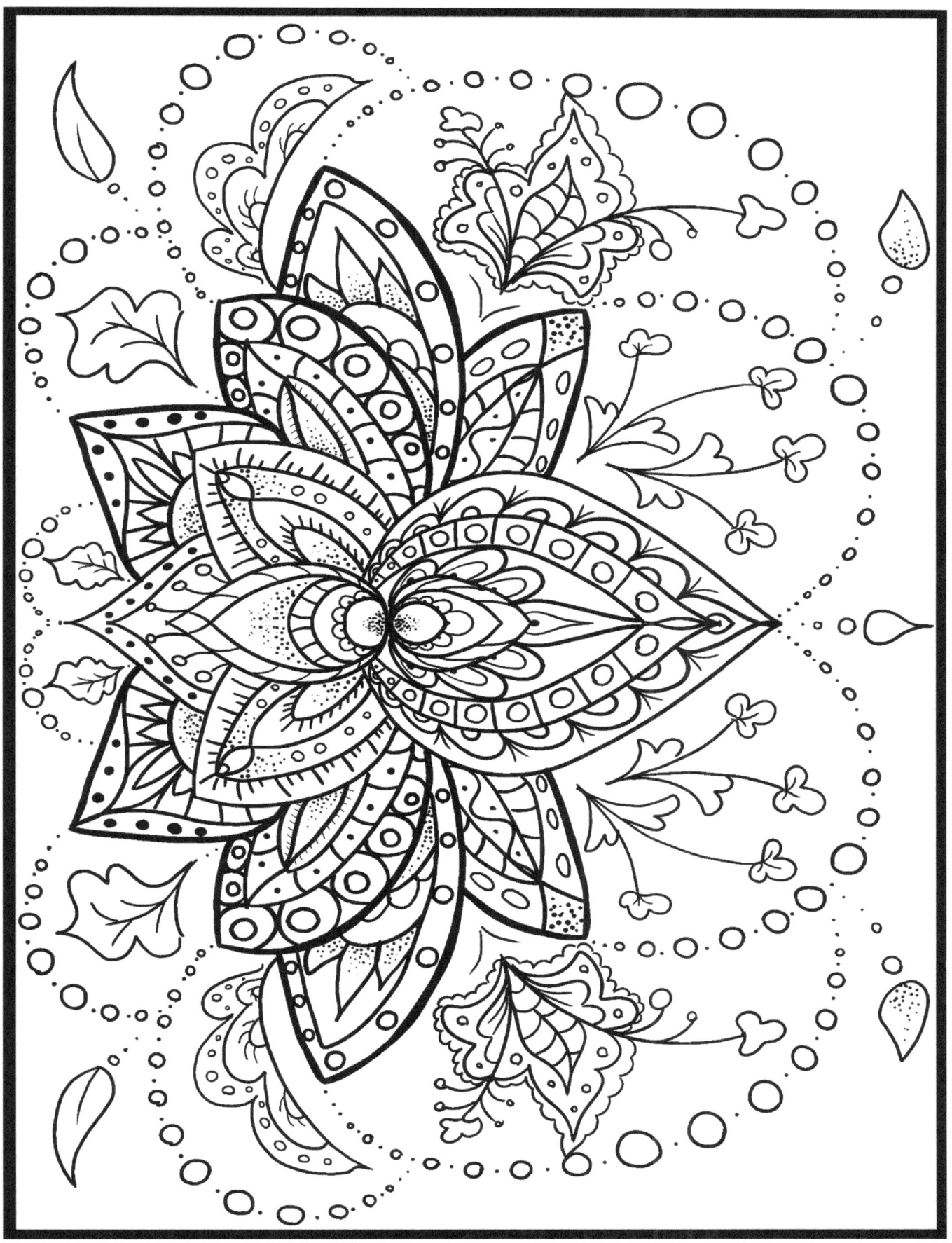

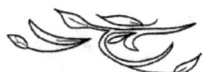

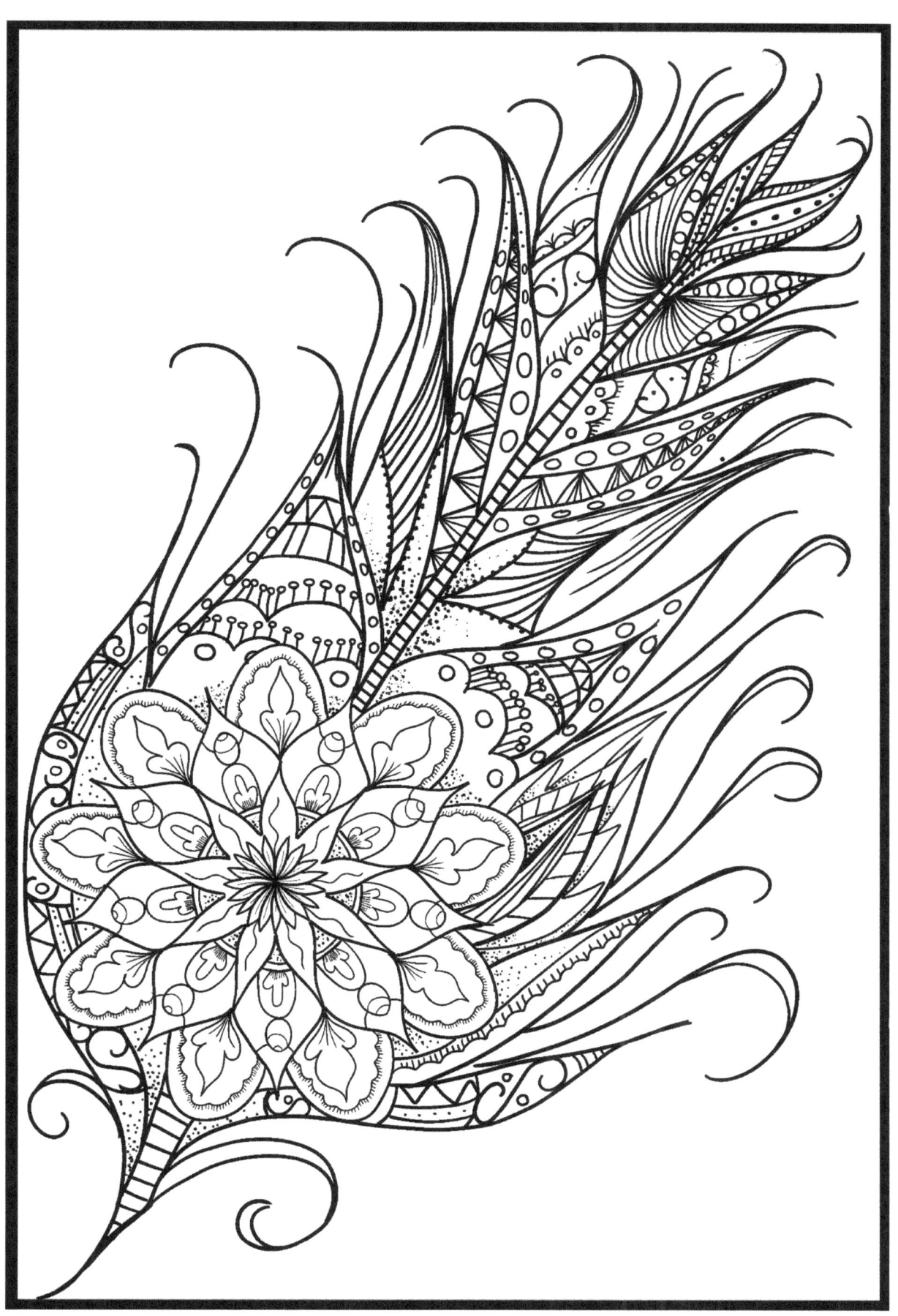

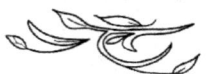

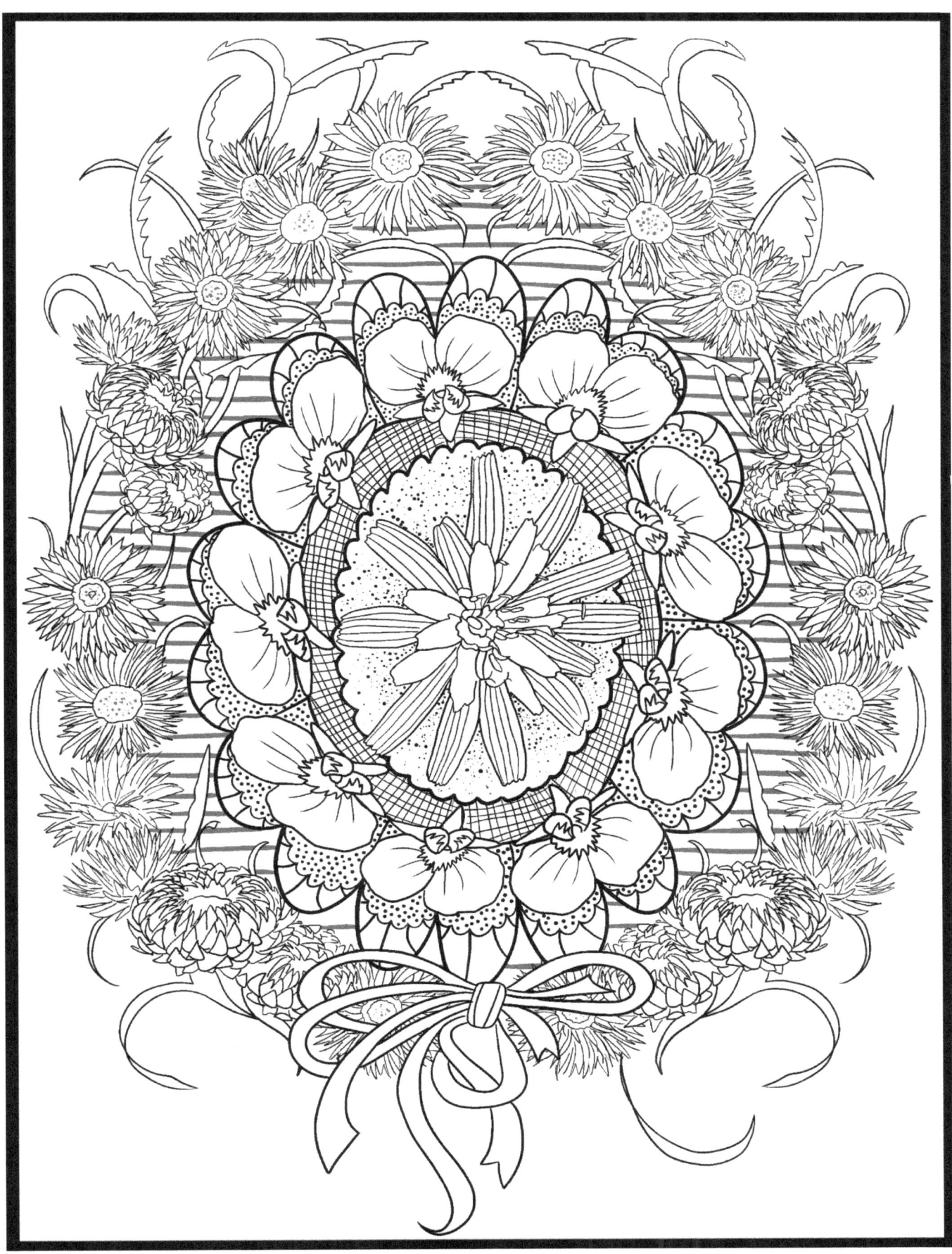

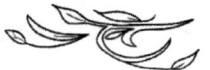

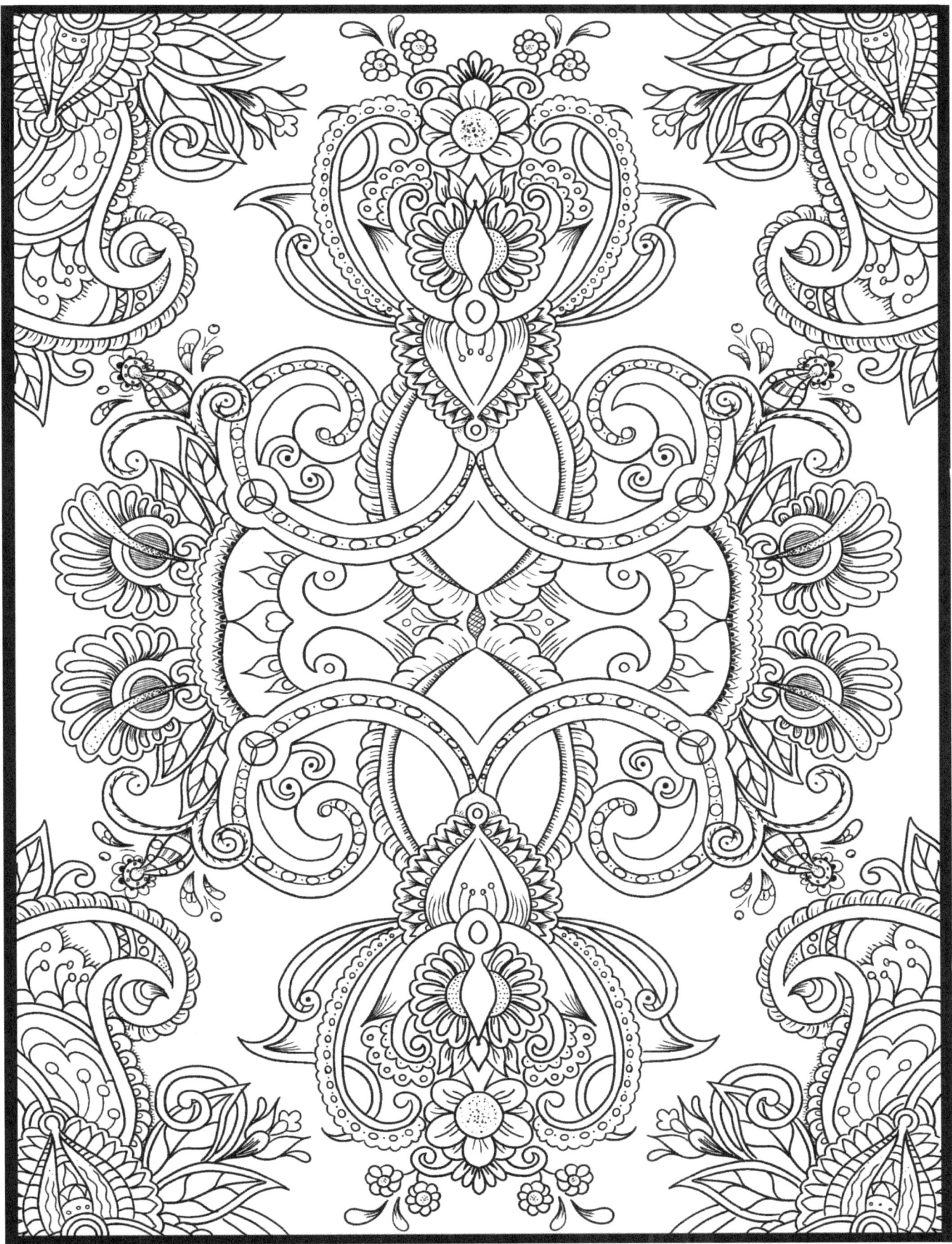

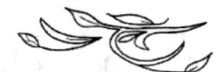

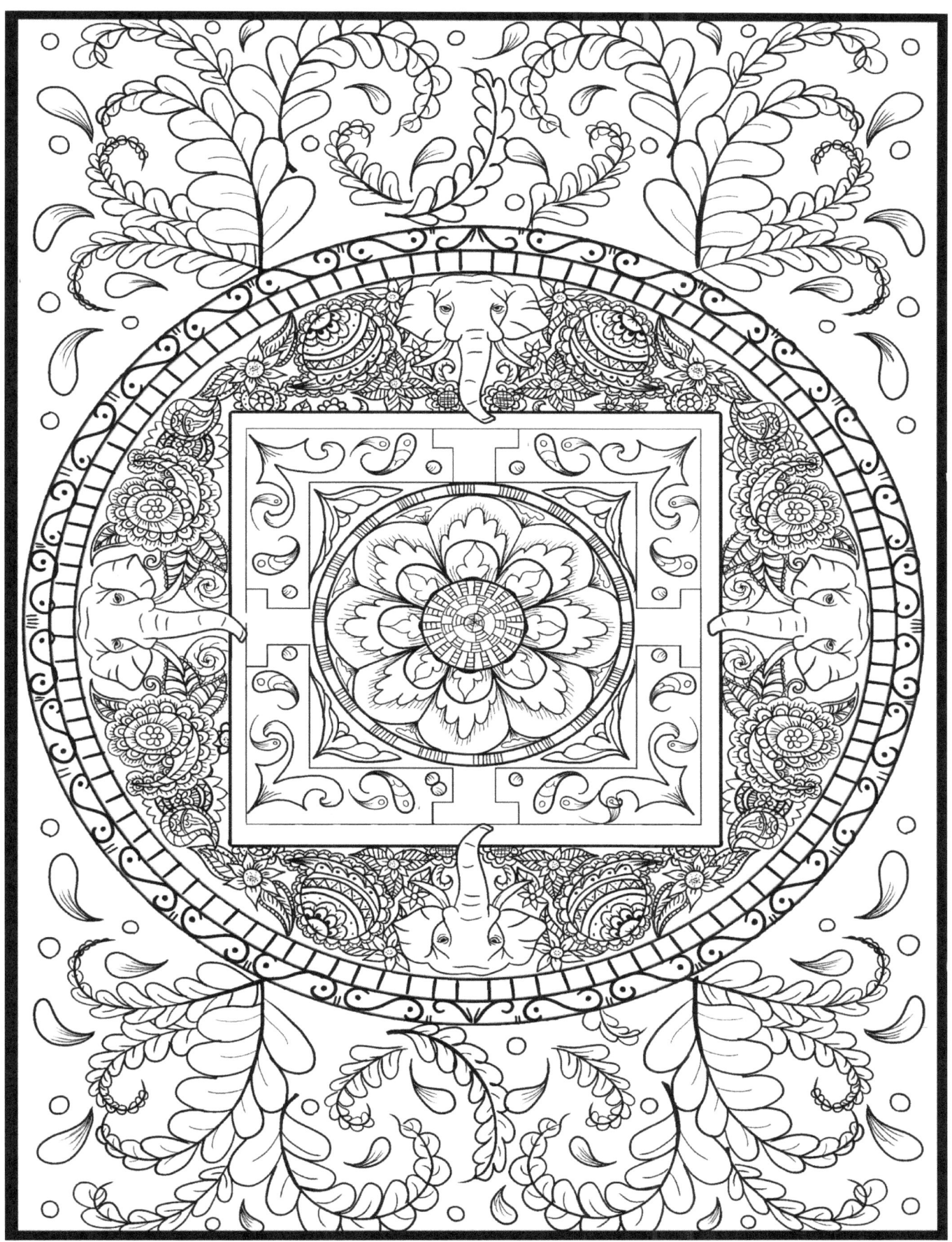

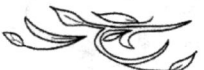

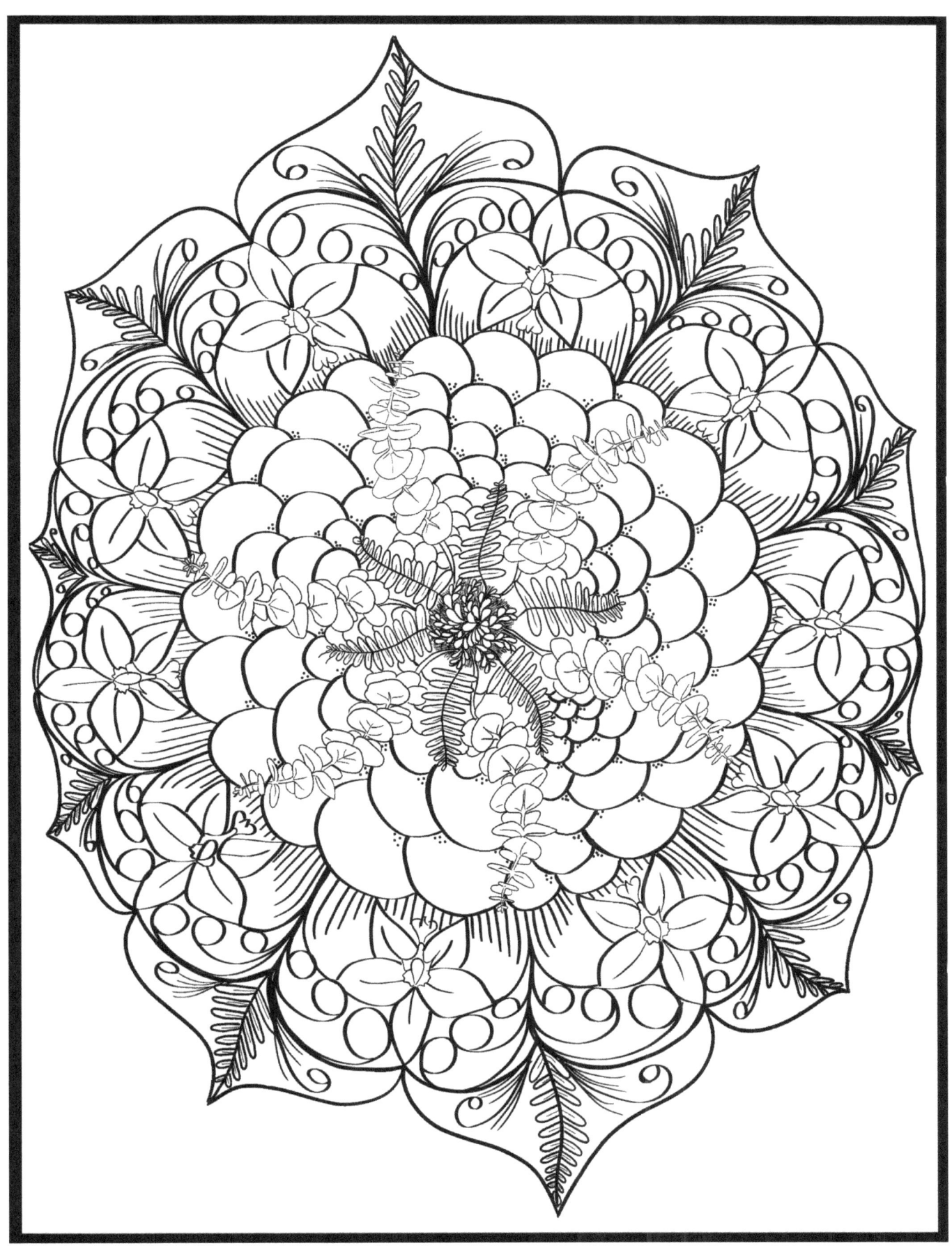

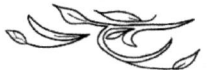

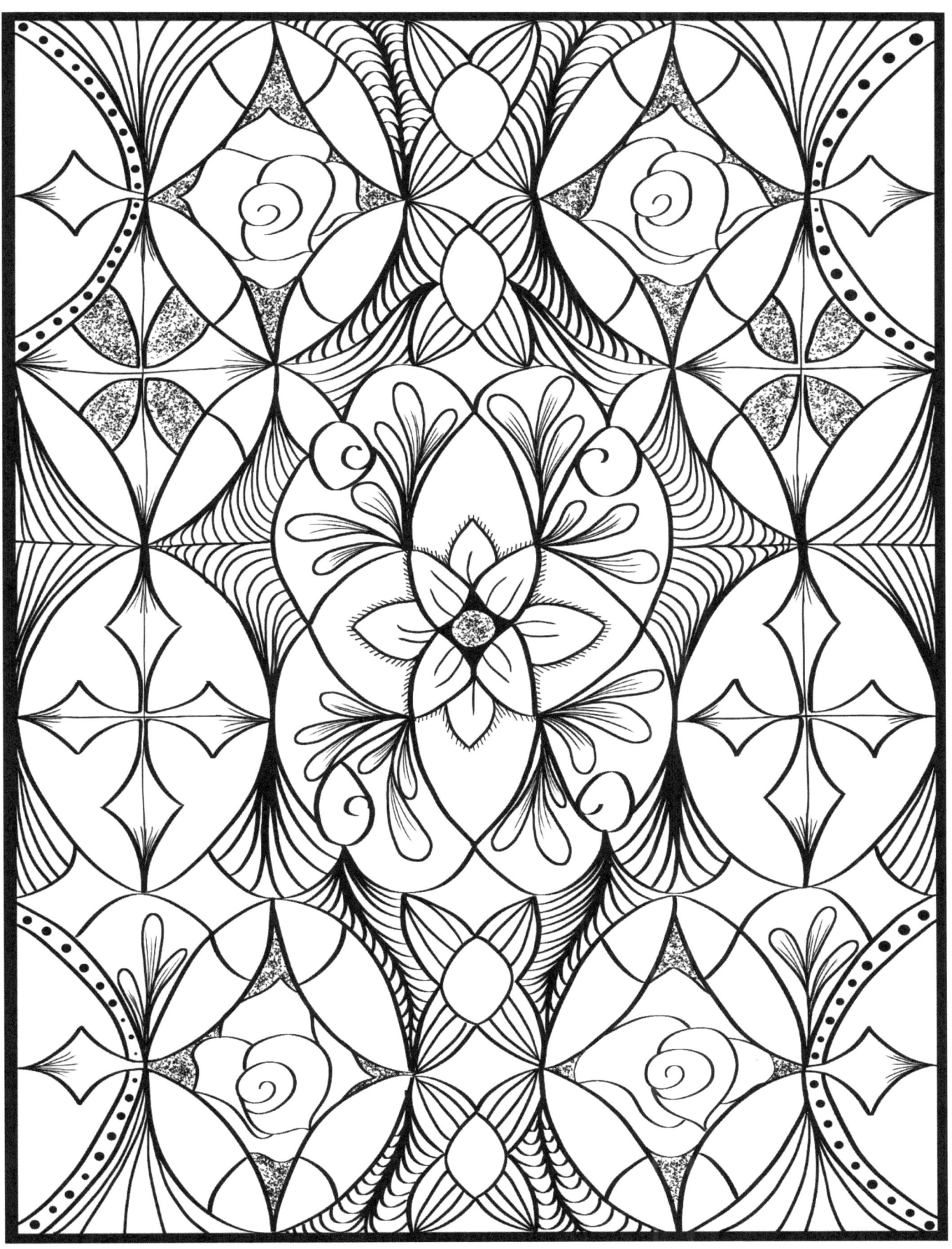

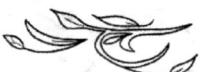

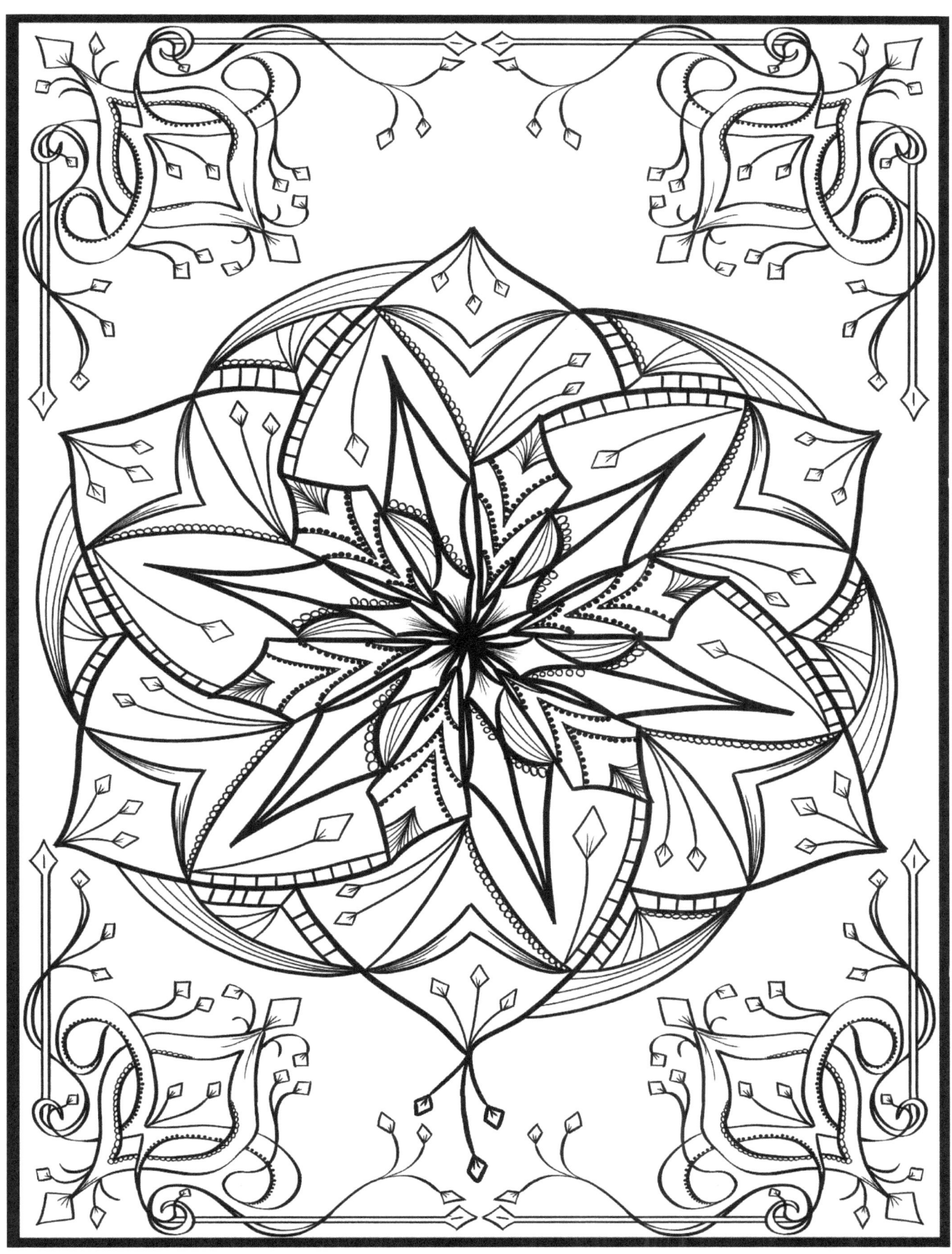

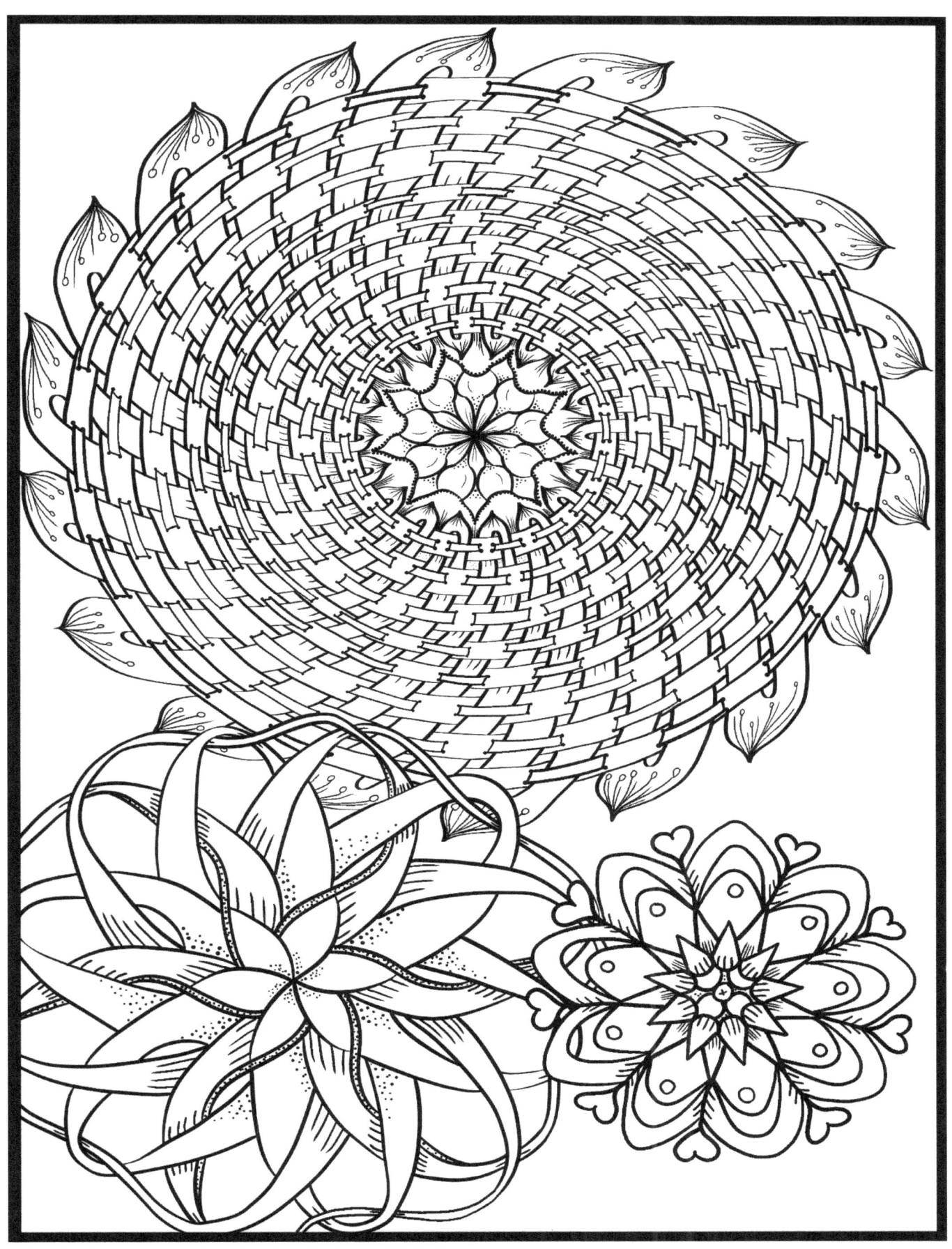

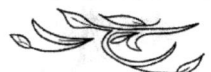

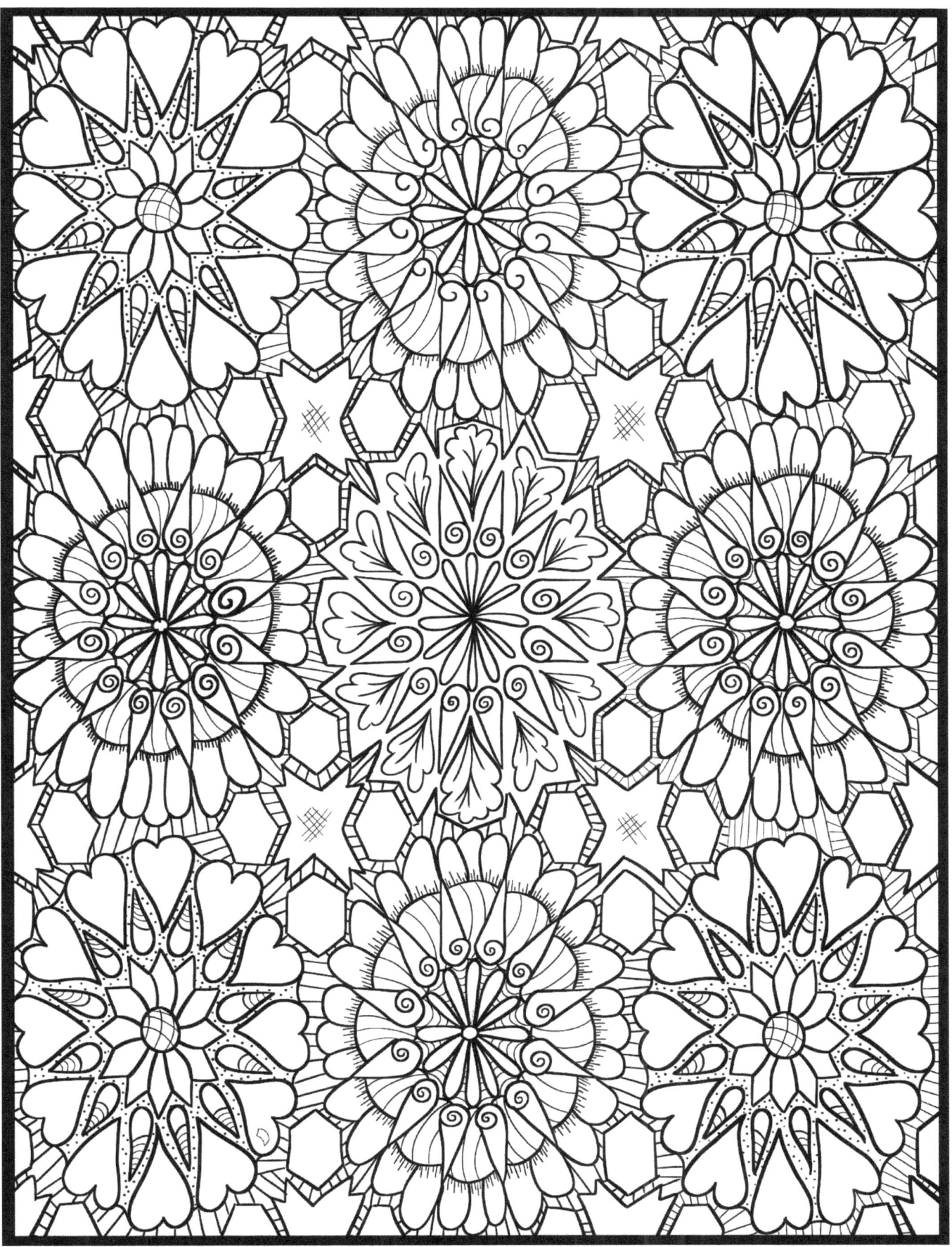

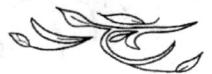

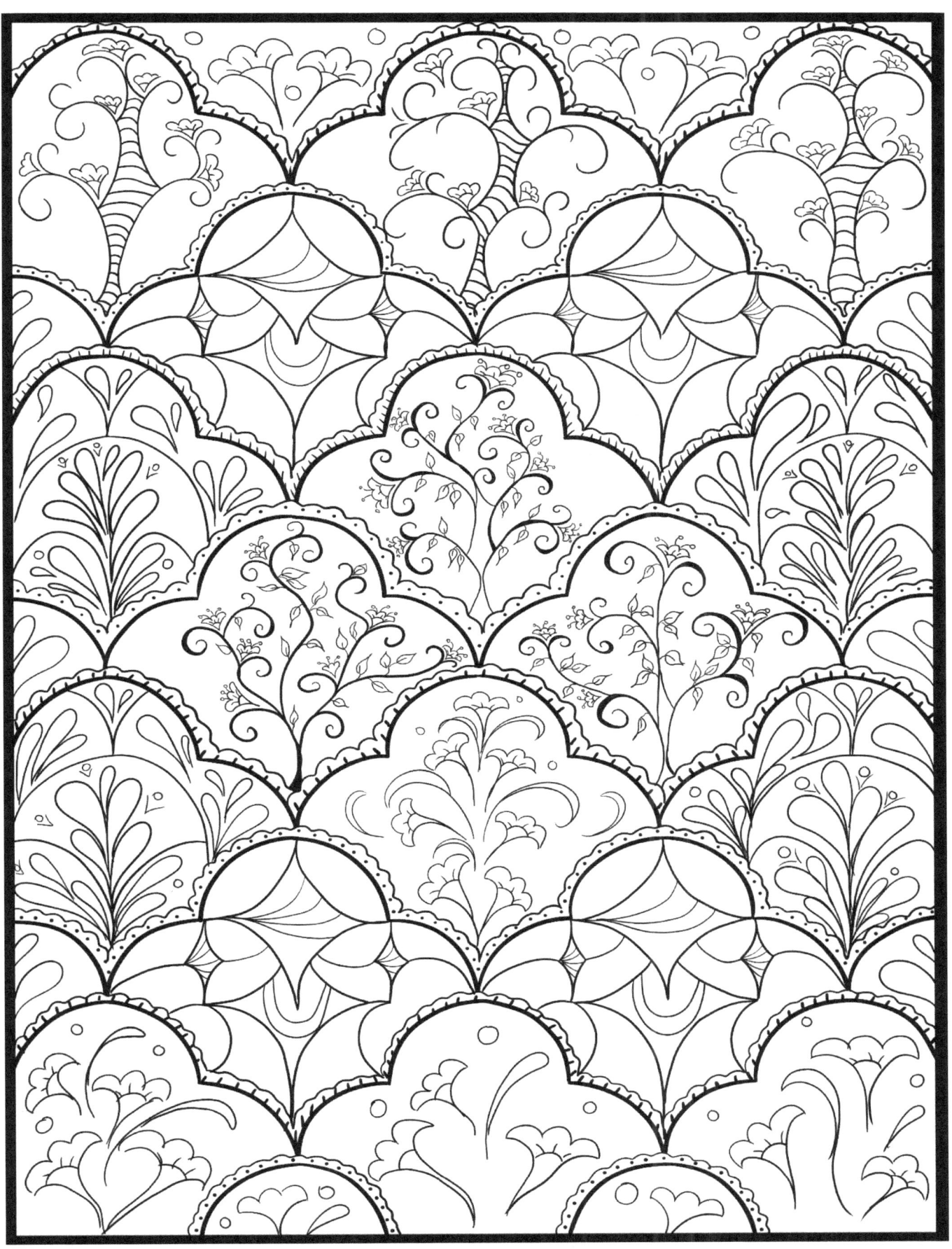

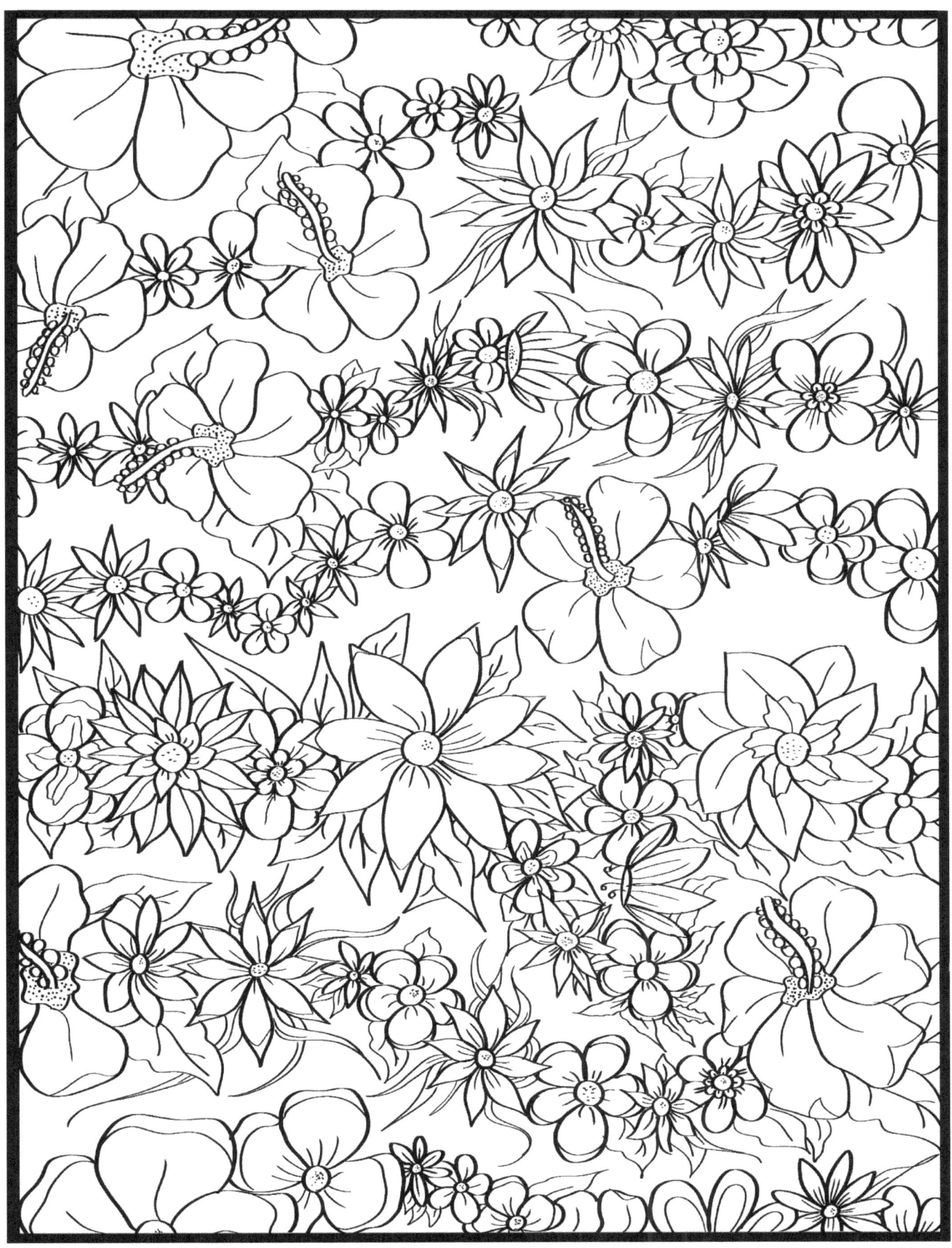

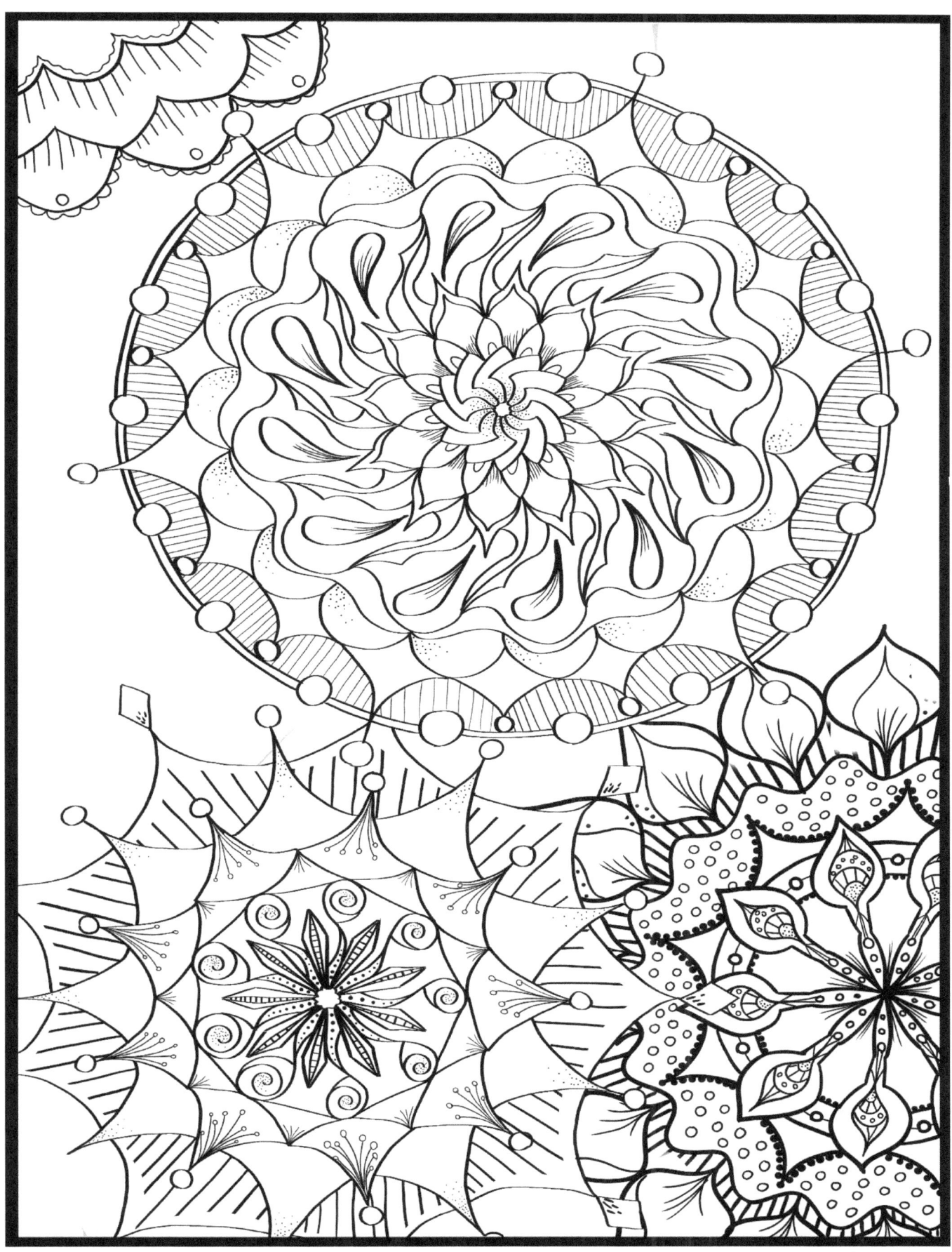

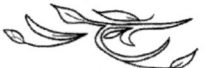

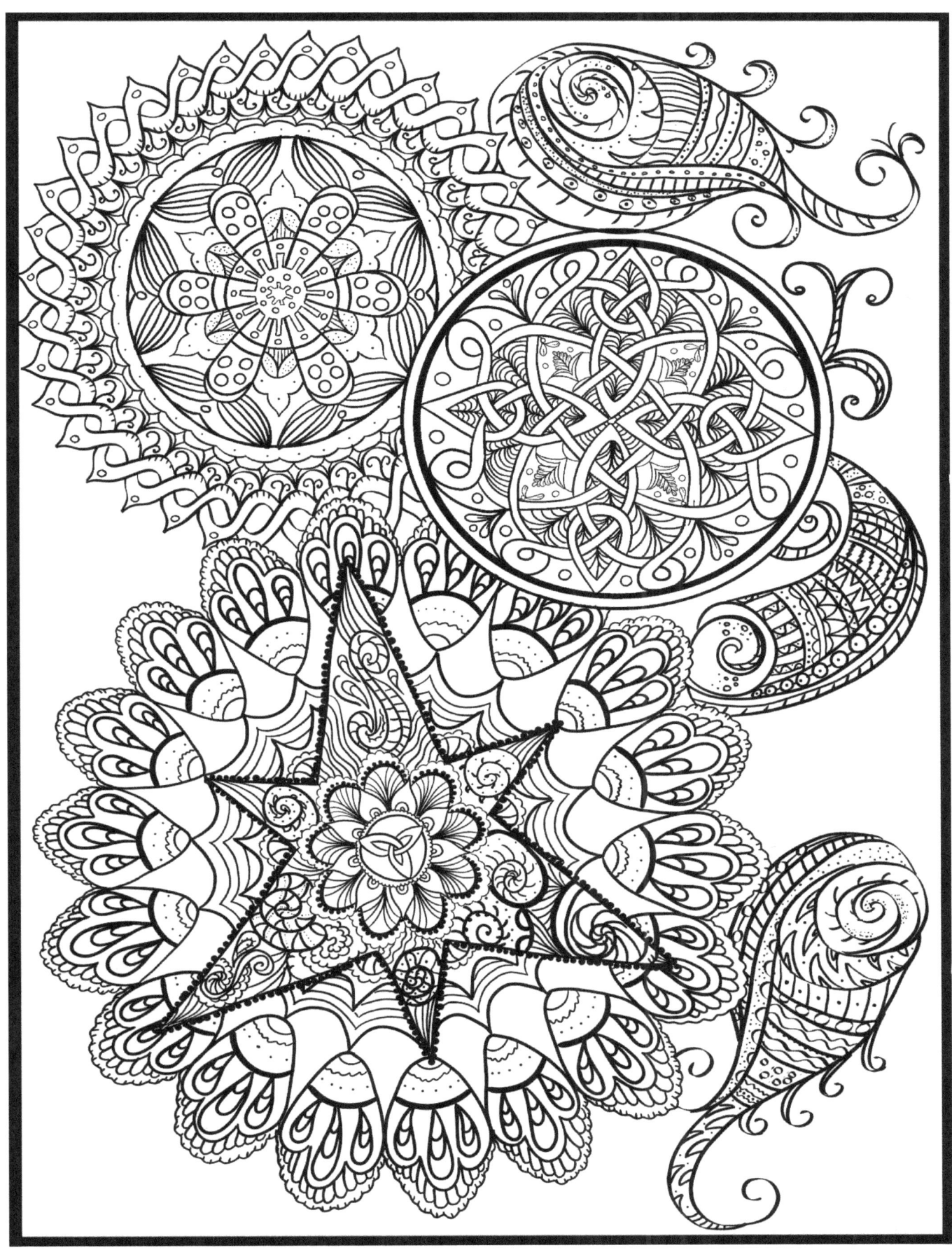

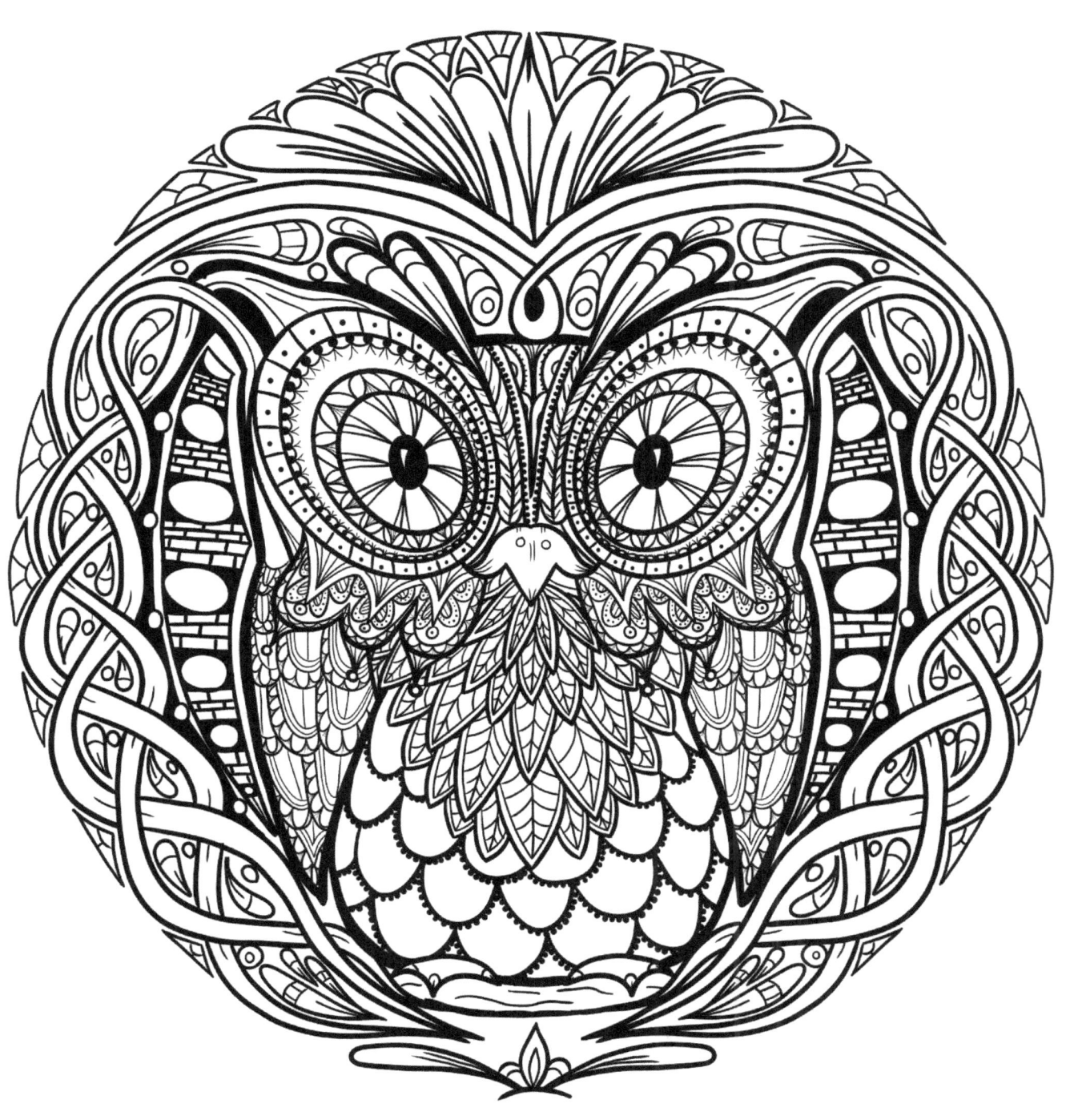

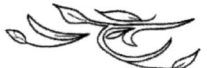

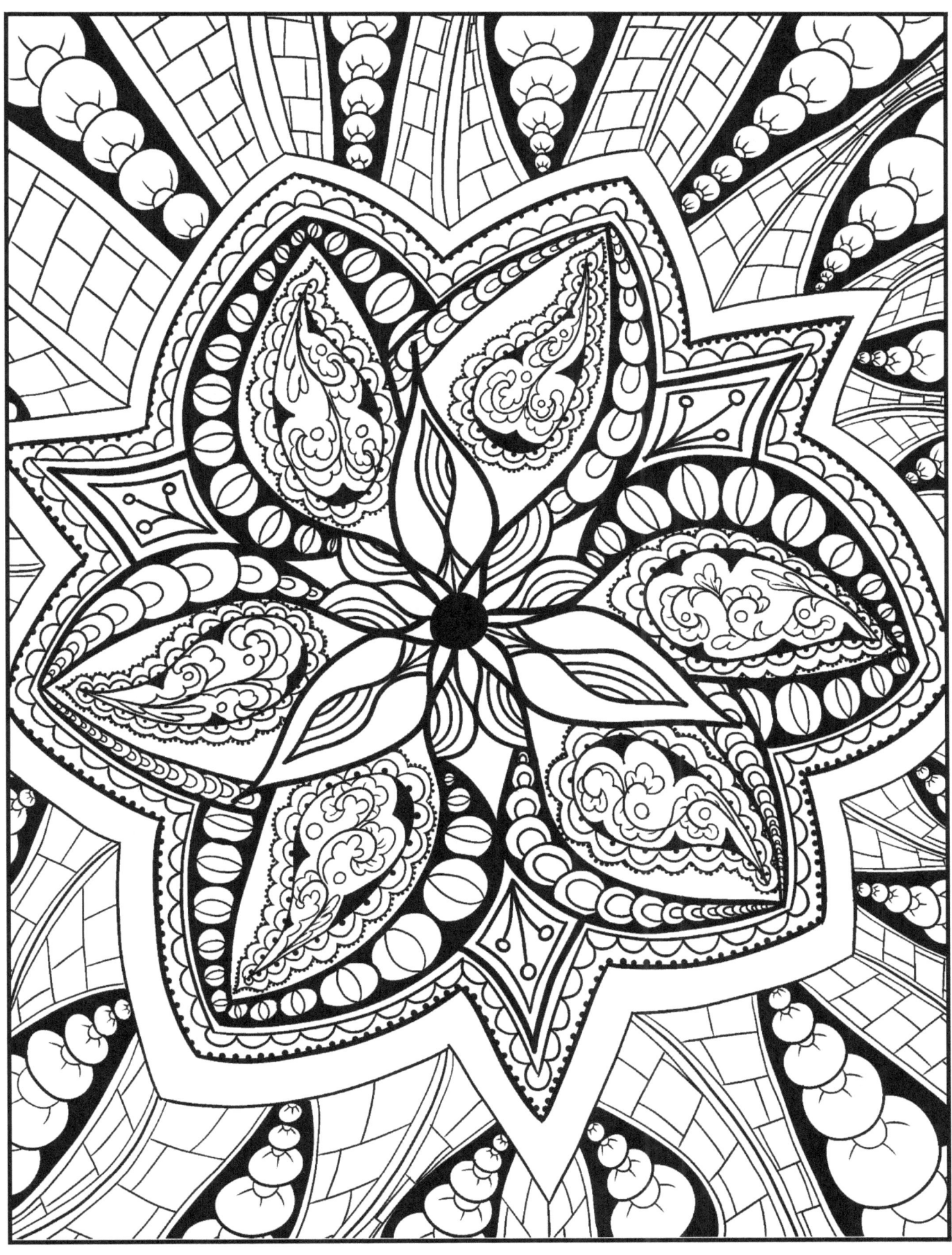

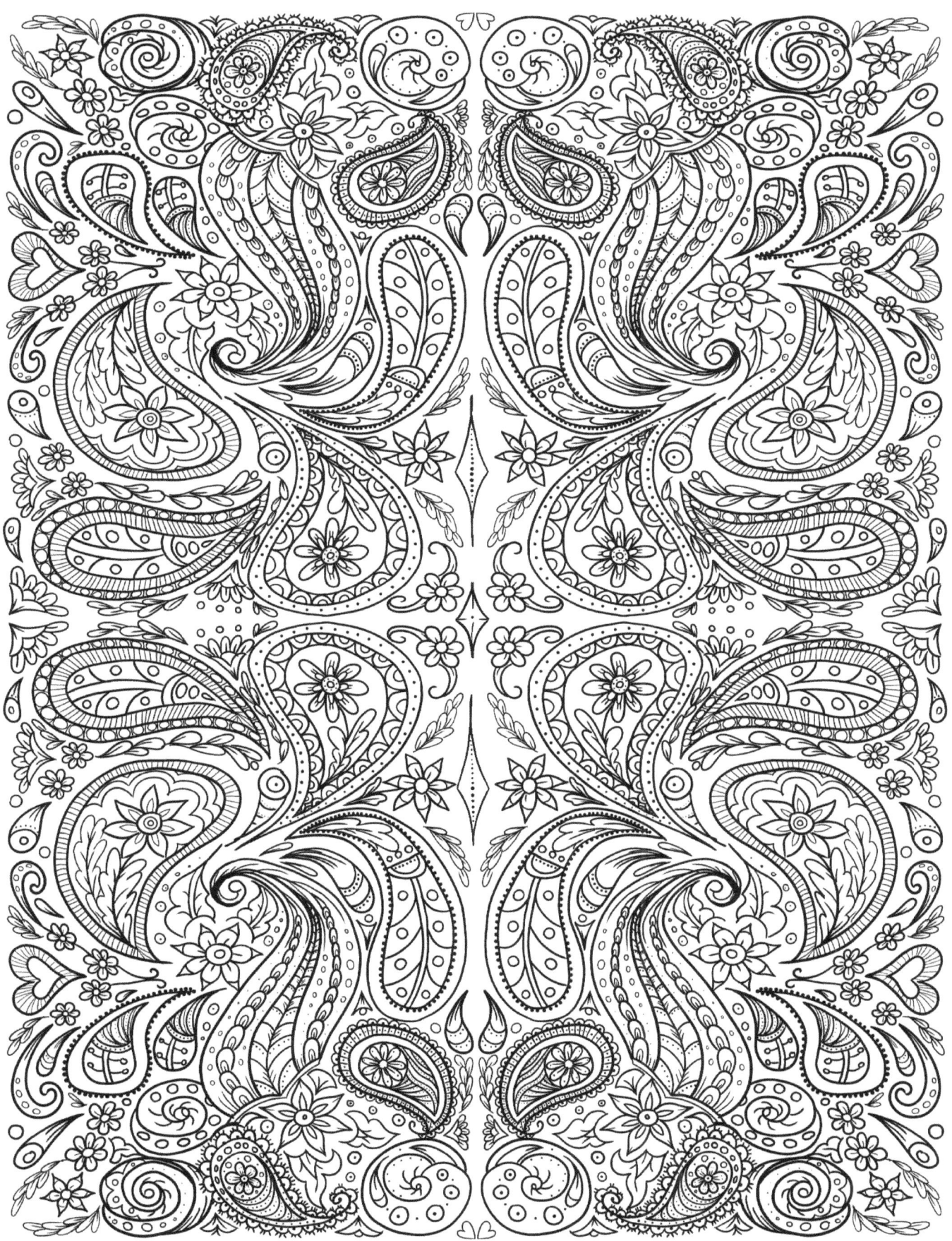

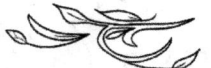

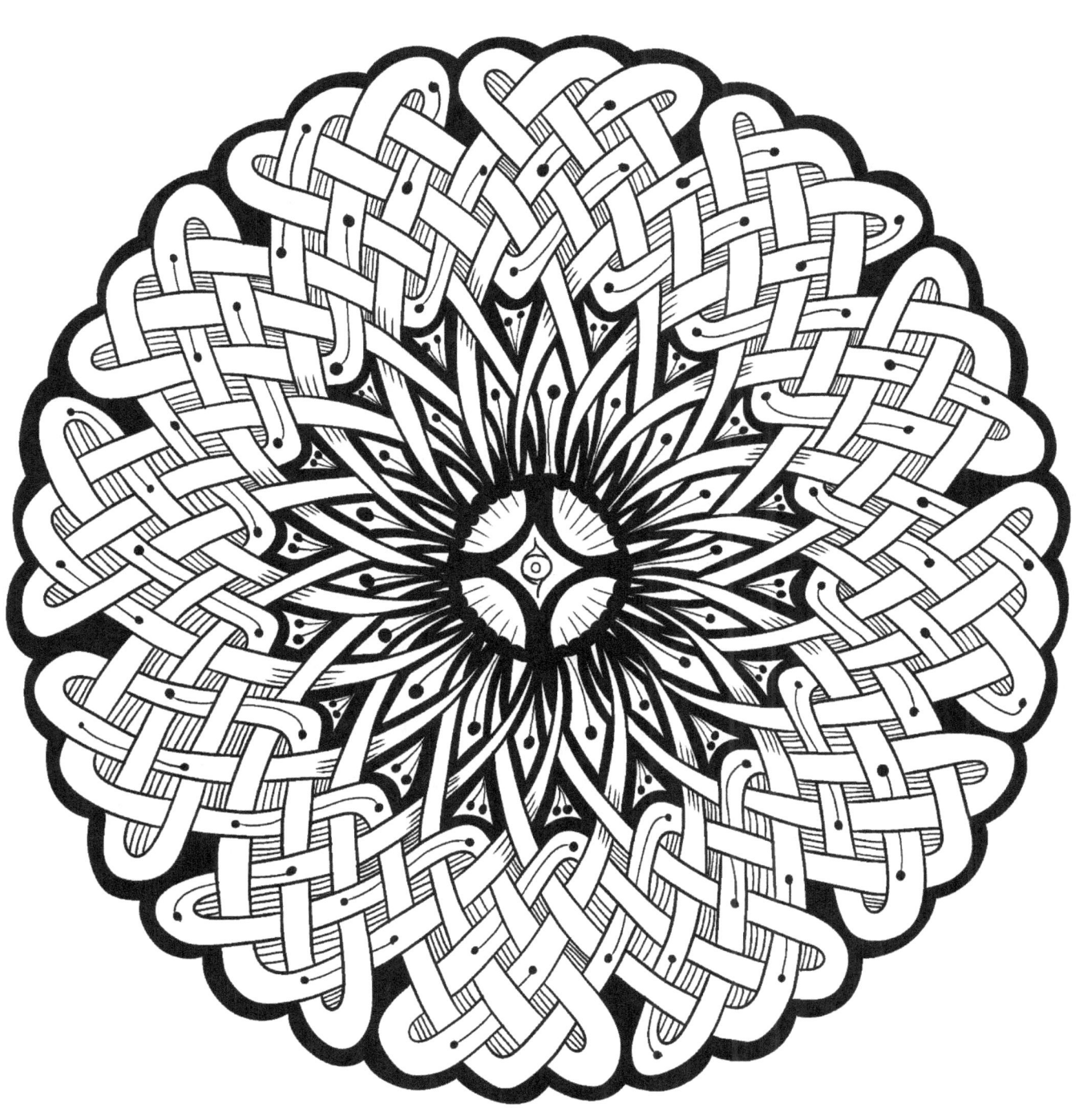

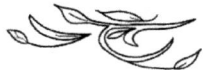

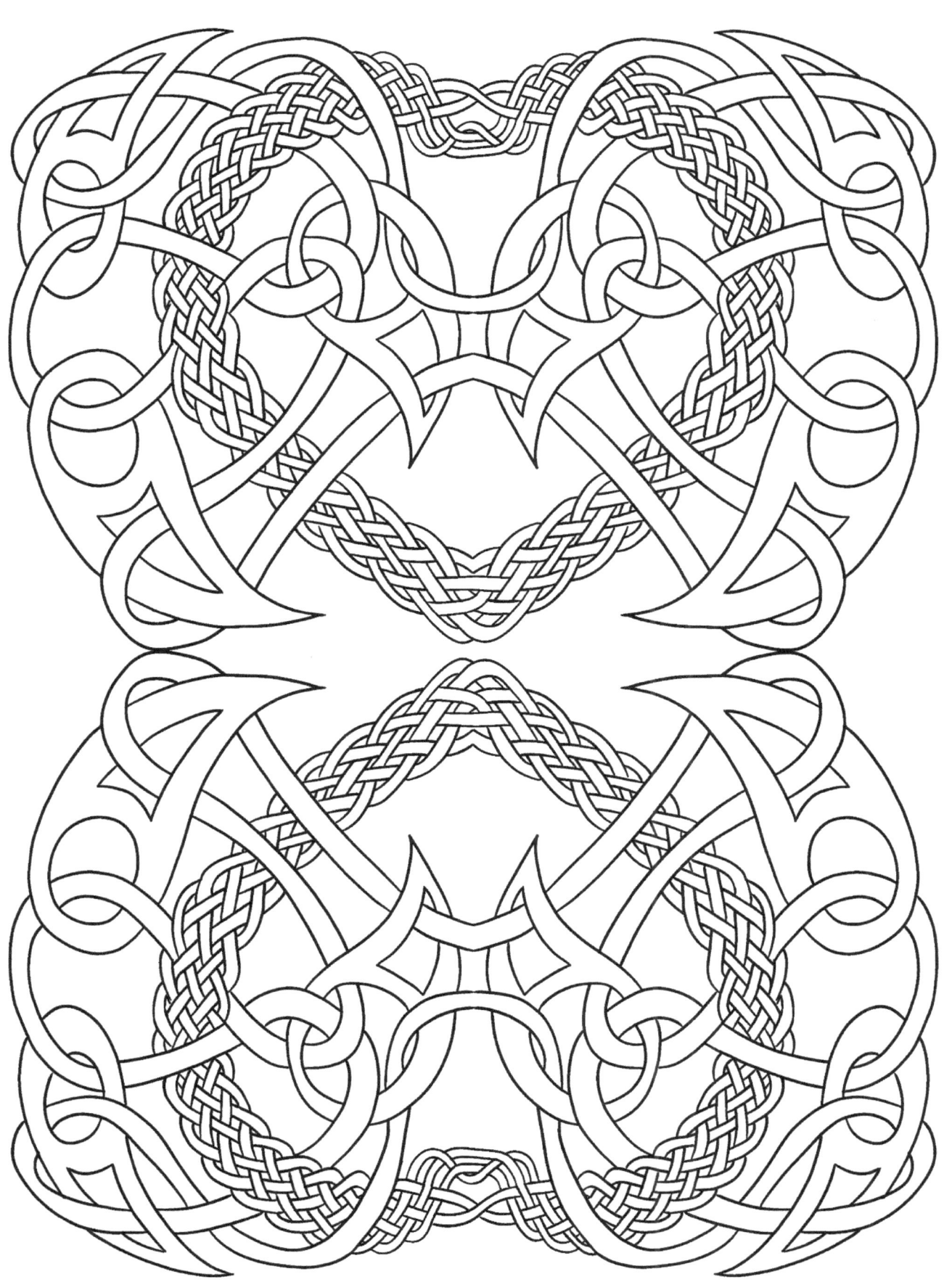

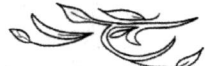

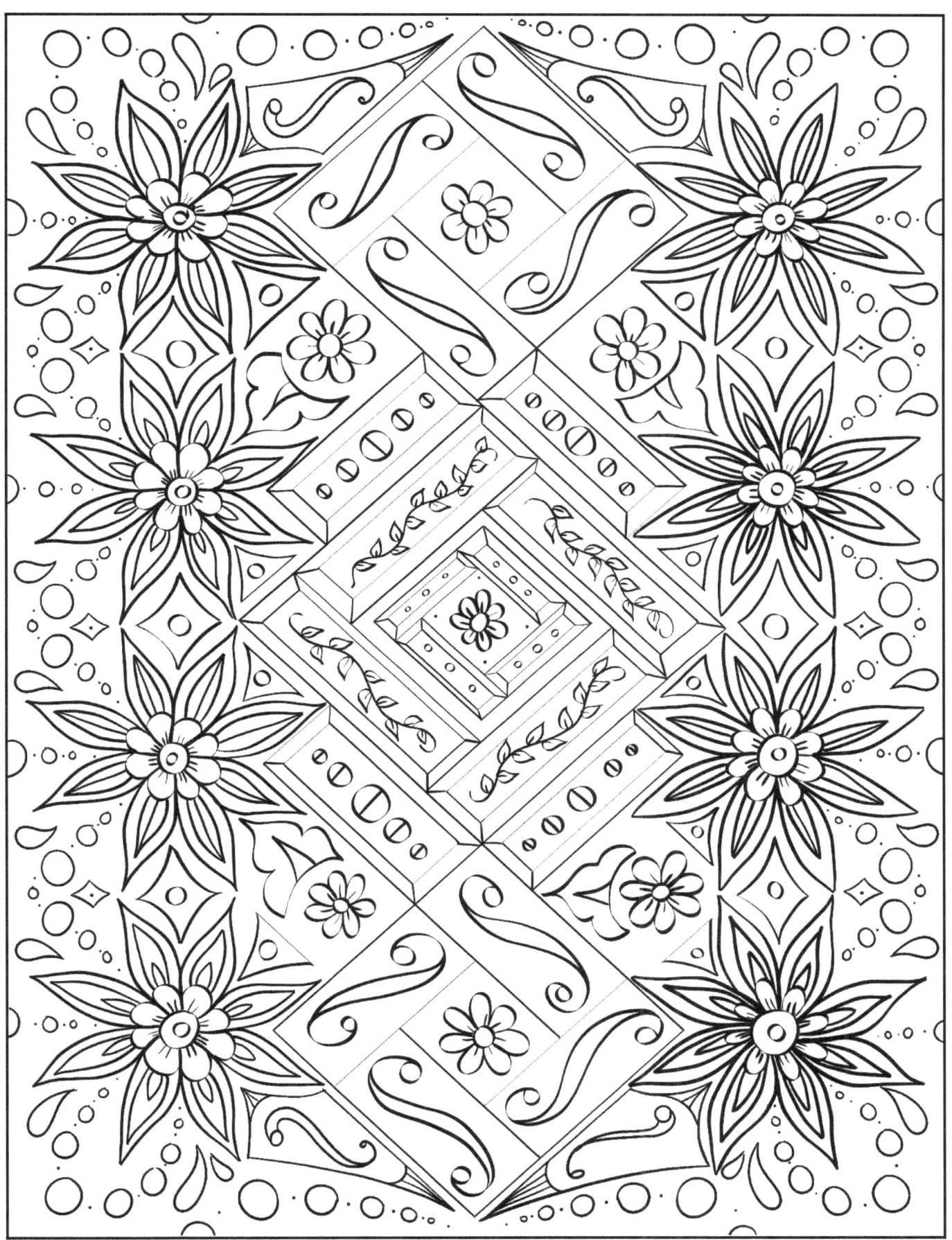

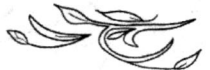

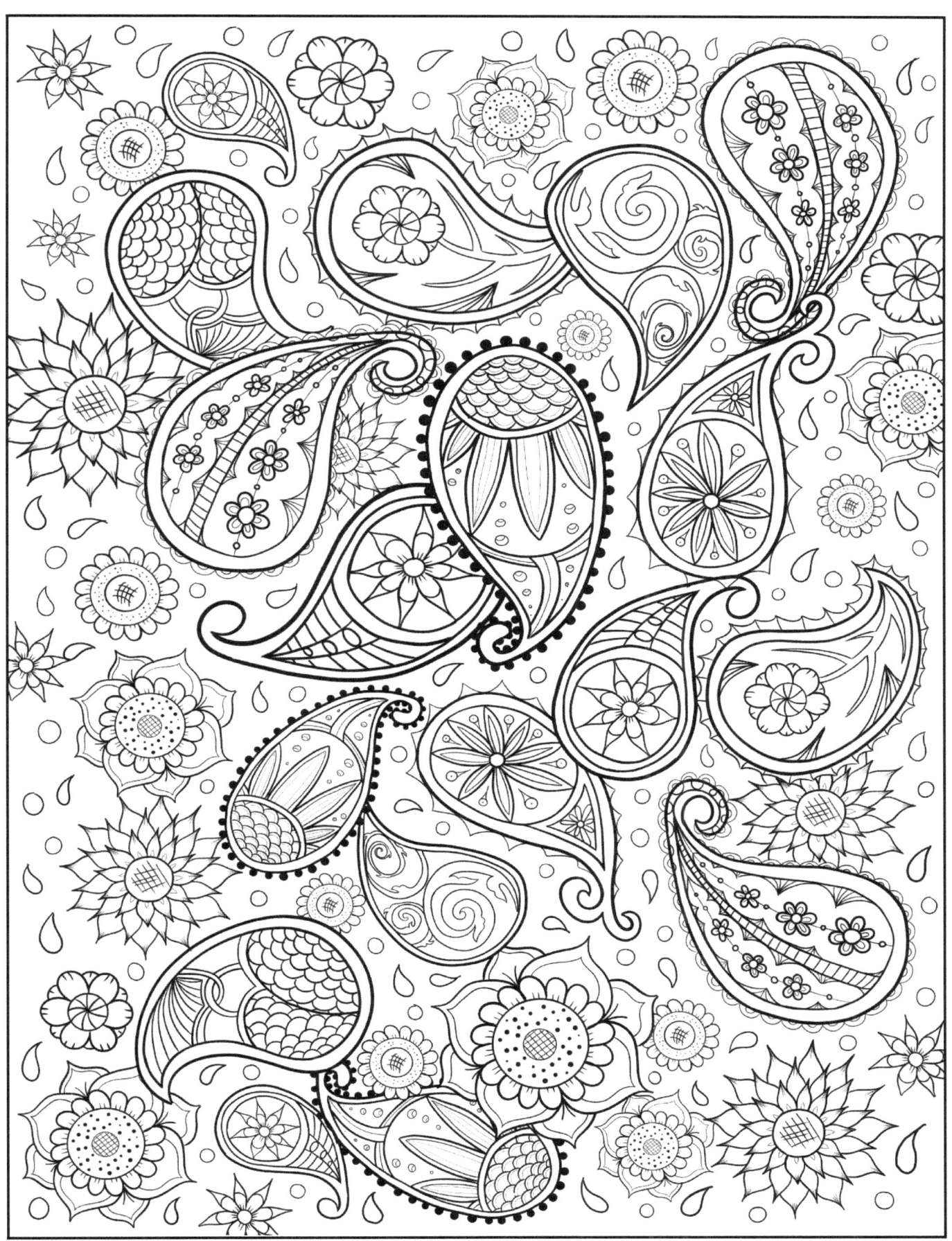

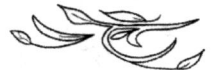

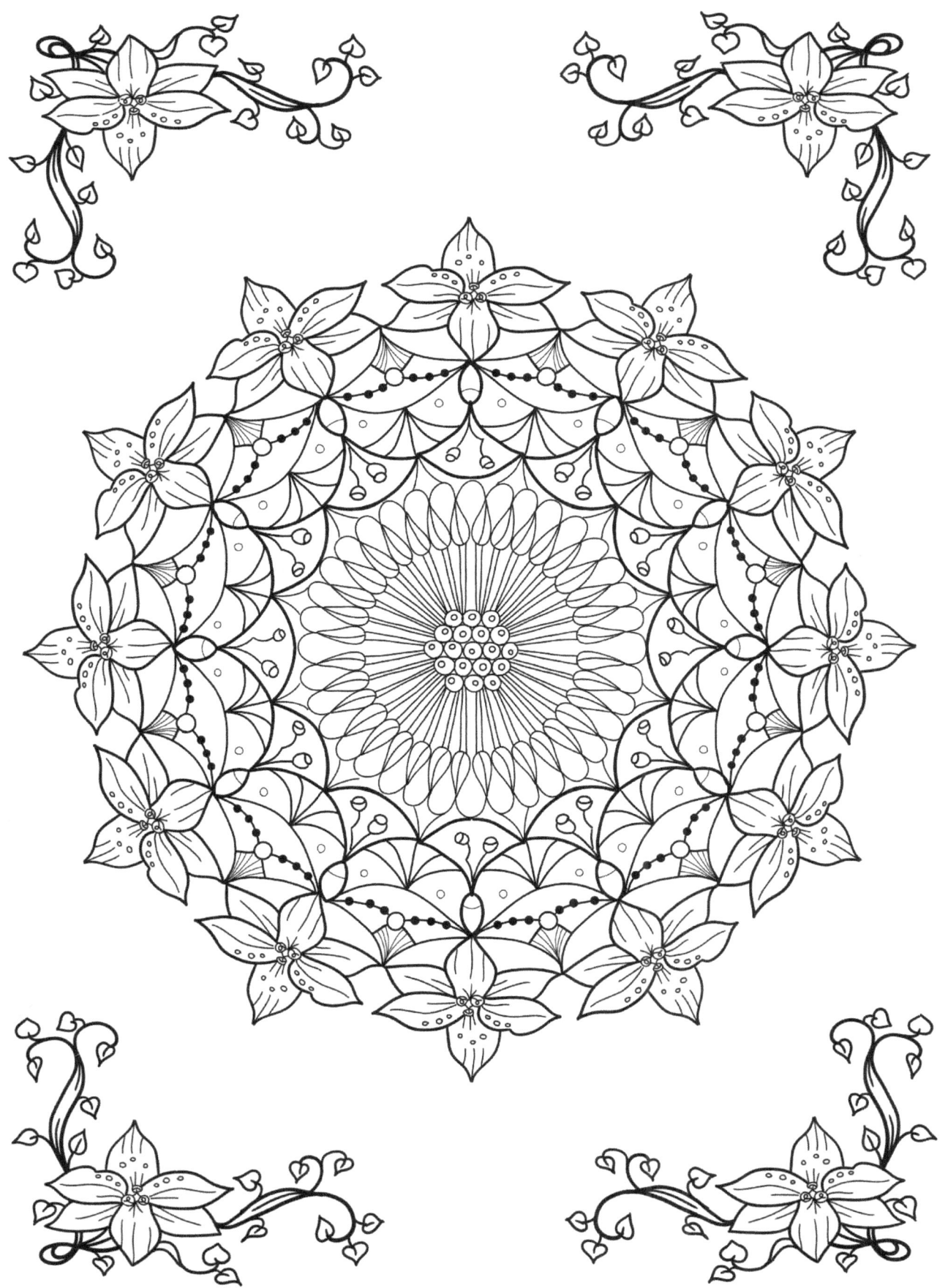

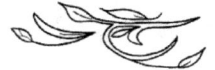

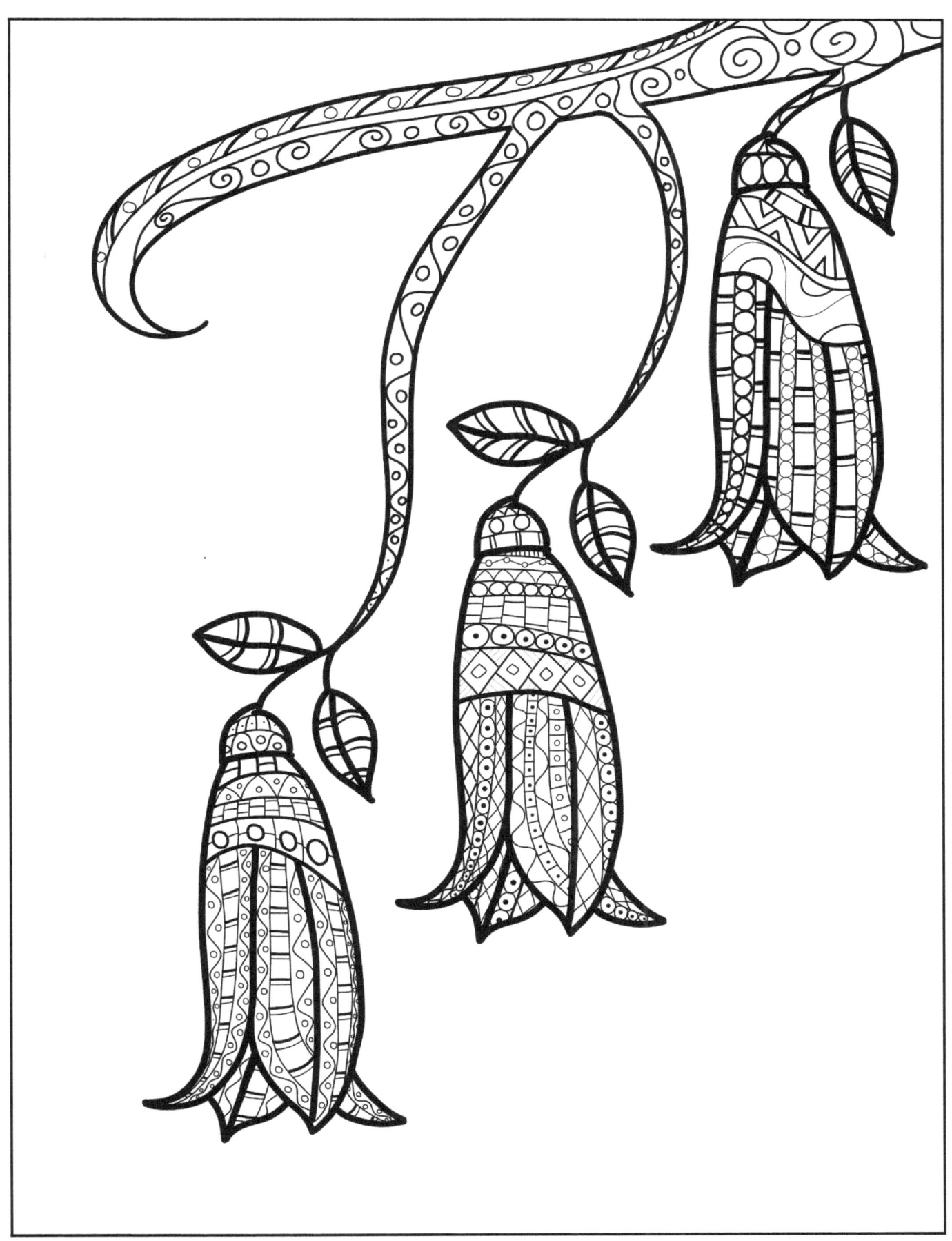

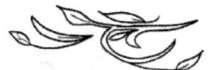

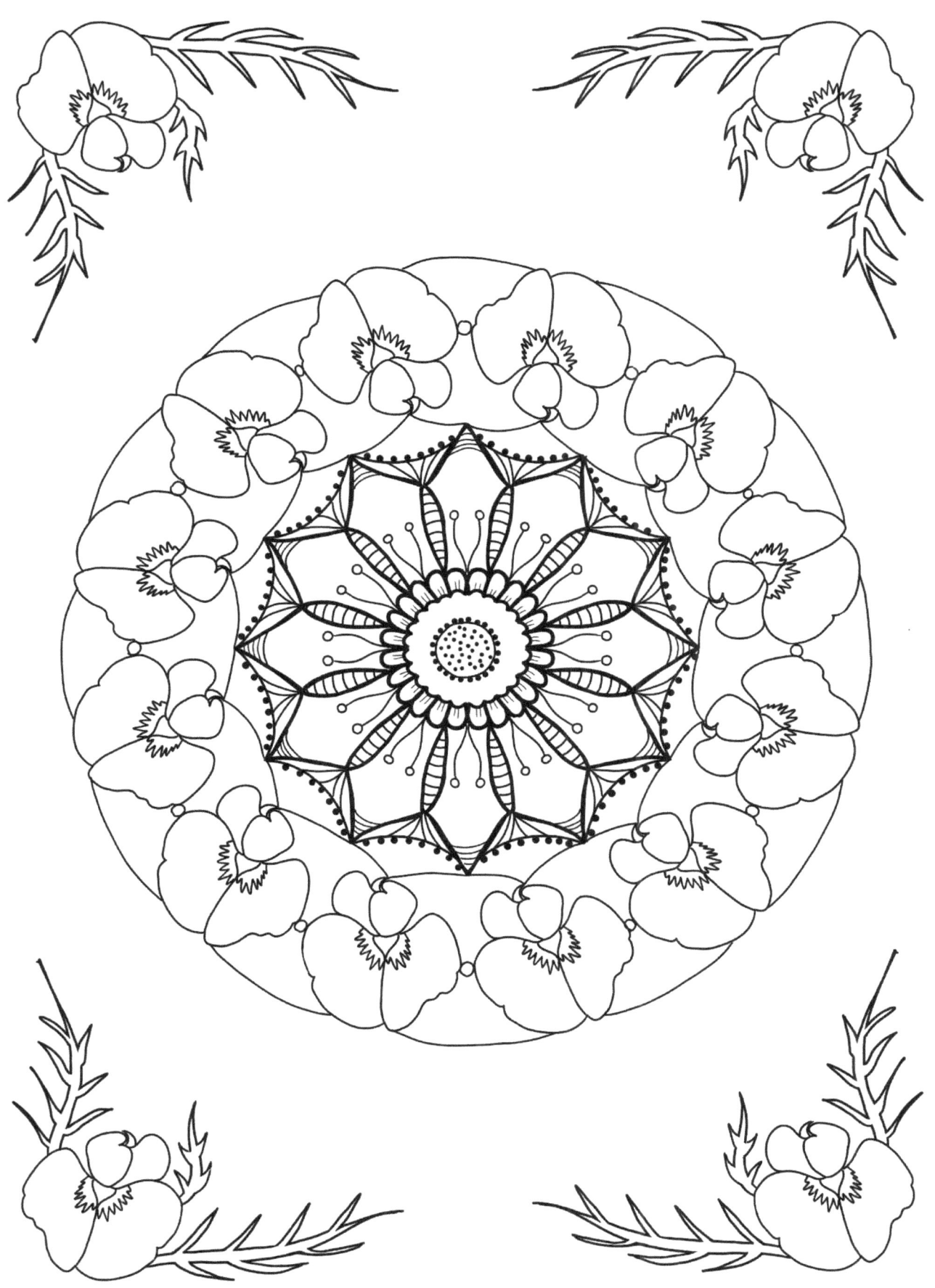

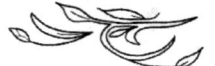

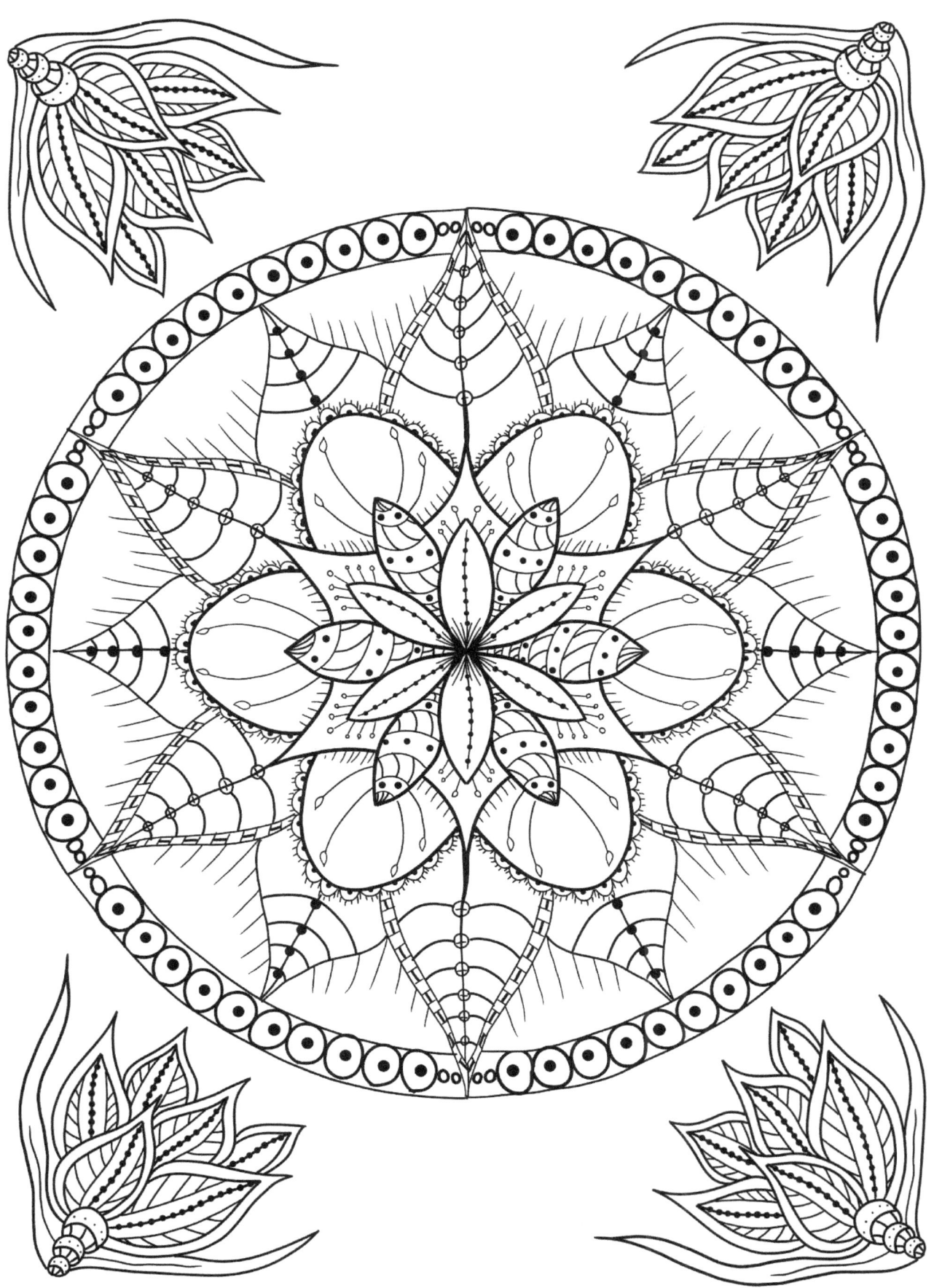